CULTURES OF THE WORLD
Hungary

Cavendish
Square

New York

Published in 2016 by Cavendish Square Publishing, LLC
243 5th Avenue, Suite 136, New York, NY 10016
Copyright © 2016 by Cavendish Square Publishing, LLC
First Edition

Website: cavendishsq.com

This publication represents the opinions and views of the author based on his or her personal experience, knowledge, and research. The information in this book serves as a general guide only. The author and publisher have used their best efforts in preparing this book and disclaim liability rising directly or indirectly from the use and application of this book.

CPSIA Compliance Information: Batch #WS15CSQ

All websites were available and accurate when this book was sent to press.

Library of Congress Cataloging-in-Publication Data

Esbenshade, Richard S.
Hungary / Richard S. Esbenshade and Debbie Nevins.
pages cm. — (Cultures of the world)
Includes bibliographical references and index.
ISBN 978-1-50260-338-8 (hardcover) ISBN 978-1-50260-339-5 (ebook)
1. Hungary—Juvenile literature. I. Nevins, Debbie. II. Title.

DB906.E83 2015
943.9—dc23

2015004885

Writers, Richard S. Esbenshade; Debbie Nevins, third edition
Editorial Director, third edition: David McNamara
Editor, third edition: Debbie Nevins
Art Director, third edition: Jeffrey Talbot
Designer, third edition: Jessica Nevins
Production Manager, third edition Jennifer Ryder-Talbot
Cover Picture Researcher: Stephanie Fletcha
Picture Researcher, third edition: Jessica Nevins

PRECEDING PAGE
The Fisherman's Bastion on Castle Hill in Budapest offers panoramic views of the city and the Danube River below.

Printed in the United States of America

CONTENTS

HUNGARY TODAY

IN SOME WAYS, HUNGARY IS AN ISLAND. THIS MAY SEEM AN ODD description of a landlocked nation, a country with no coastline at all, but Hungary is a place unto itself. This Central European nation has one thing that no other country has—the Hungarian language, a tongue so different from any other that it's considered a "language isolate." Or a language island, one could say. This isn't quite true in the absolute sense, since linguists say Hungarian is a member of the Finno-Ugric family of languages, and distantly related to Finnish and Estonian. But even on that branch of the language family tree, Hungarian is off on its own, a twig unto itself, so to speak—with Finnish and Estonian being much closer to each other than to Hungarian. And geographically, of course, Finland and Estonia are nowhere near Hungary anyway.

Hungarians love the uniqueness of their language, and it is one of the strongest elements binding them together as a people and a culture. Some Hungarians even go so far as to take umbrage with the idea that their language is a twig connected to the Finno-Ugric branch. In their view, Hungarian is its own freestanding tree. The Ugric part of that Finno-Ugric language family comes from a tiny region in the Ural

This shining cityscape shows the capital of Hungary straddling the Danube River.

Mountains of Russia, near the European-Asian border. Historians believe the Magyar tribes who settled in the region of today's Hungary more than a thousand years ago originally came from that place. Indeed, the Khanty and Mansi languages native to that region are closer to Hungarian than any others, but they are spoken by so few people as to be nearly extinct. They are not all that similar to Hungarian anyway—but then, a thousand years of separation can do that. However, some Hungarians discard this "Asiatic tribes" theory of their origins. Instead, they embrace an alternative ethno-linguistic theory that says they evolved from ancient Sumerian roots, which perhaps seems a more noble history. (Most historians and linguistics disagree.)

Whatever the reasons, Hungary today seems just a bit different or apart from other European nations. Some call it special or distinctive; others say it's exotic. Still others, looking at Hungary from a political point of view, say it's dangerous. (More on that later.)

Some observers say Hungary has a national chip on its shoulder. The people suffer from the perception that as a nationality they are underestimated and undervalued. Some Hungarians even think there's an international conspiracy to keep them down. Throughout history, Hungary has been bullied and dominated by outside powers. For one thing, Hungarians are still angry about the Treaty of Trianon that, in 1920, redrew the boundaries of the new, independent state of Hungary. The World War I peace treaty chopped off great sections of the old Hungarian Kingdom and gave them to neighboring countries. Transylvania, for example, was given to Romania, though enclaves of ethnic Hungarians live there (and speak their beloved Hungarian there) to this day. The new borders left Hungary landlocked and much smaller—and left the people of Hungary very bitter indeed. Even now, a century later, some Hungarians drive around with a *Nagymagyarország* sticker on their car, which means "Great Hungary" or "Big Hungary." The word is overlaid on a map showing the country with its pre-1920 boundaries.

One of the drivers seen sporting that bumper sticker is Viktor Orbán, the prime minister of Hungary since 2010. The success of Orbán and his conservative Fidesz party in two parliamentary election cycles indicates Hungary's strong political shift to the right. The party's victory in 2010 was large enough that it could rewrite the Constitution with no input from other political parties, and that's exactly what it did.

Hungarians in Budapest hold Hungarian and Transylvanian flags as they demonstrate for the autonomy of Transylvania from Romania in 2013.

In 2015, thousands of people gather outside the Parliament Building in Budapest, demanding "a European Hungary." They are calling for Prime Minister Viktor Orbán to resign.

Orbán has taken a confrontational, go-it-alone stance toward the European Union, which it joined in 2004, demonstrating some of that characteristic Hungarian resistance and loner attitude. He has seemed, to many Western observers, to be giving the West the cold shoulder while warming up to Russia's Vladimir Putin. For a member nation of NATO, and a country that suffered greatly under the authoritarianism of the Soviet Union, this behavior certainly raised some nervous eyebrows across Europe and beyond.

After all, in 2014, Russia annexed the Crimea in Ukraine, which seemed to indicate an expansionist frame of mind on Putin's part. And in his public statements, Orbán has been advocating a shift away from democracy and toward "a different, special, national approach" toward governing, which seems to many pundits to mean "more authoritarian." Plenty of Hungarians have been nervous as well. In February 2015, thousands of protesters took to the streets of Budapest for a "Spring Comes, Orbán Goes" rally.

Meanwhile, the nationalist, even-farther-right Jobbik party has won the support of many Hungarians, particularly the young. Following the 2014 elections, Jobbik held 43 out of 386 seats in the Hungarian parliament. This party is widely seen as anti-immigrant, anti-Semitic, and anti-Roma, a minority people, also called Gypsies, who live throughout Eastern Europe.

One reason this alarms many people, both Hungarians and outside observers, is the memory of the role Hungary played in the Holocaust and World War II, sending thousands of Jews and Roma to their deaths at the hands of the Nazis. In 2014, Csaba Korosi, the Hungarian ambassador to the United Nations, admitted and apologized for Hungary's complicity in the Holocaust. This was the first time the country apologized for its involvement. This was noteworthy, as Hungary has historically shown a tendency to downplay its national role in the genocide, preferring to blame others and portray itself as a passive victim as well.

Some people worry that Hungary's shift to the authoritarian right is a dangerous precedent that could spread throughout Europe. Others think it's a passing phase, and that as the right proves itself incapable of solving Hungary's problems, the tide will turn once more.

School children hold a poster showing the Jewish deportation during WWII, to protest against the far-right Jobbik party.

For many Hungarians, it's all just politics and life goes on. After all, the country is connected to the rest of the world through technology in ways it never was before. Hungary is still making the difficult transition from the bad old days of Communism and Soviet dominance to being a truly independent, twenty-first century nation. The country is trying to figure out what it means to be Hungarian and what Hungary's place in the world is; what it can be, and what it should be. Like any other country, it has problems to solve, but it also has a heritage of beautiful places, marvelous things, and good people on which to base a healthy and productive national pride.

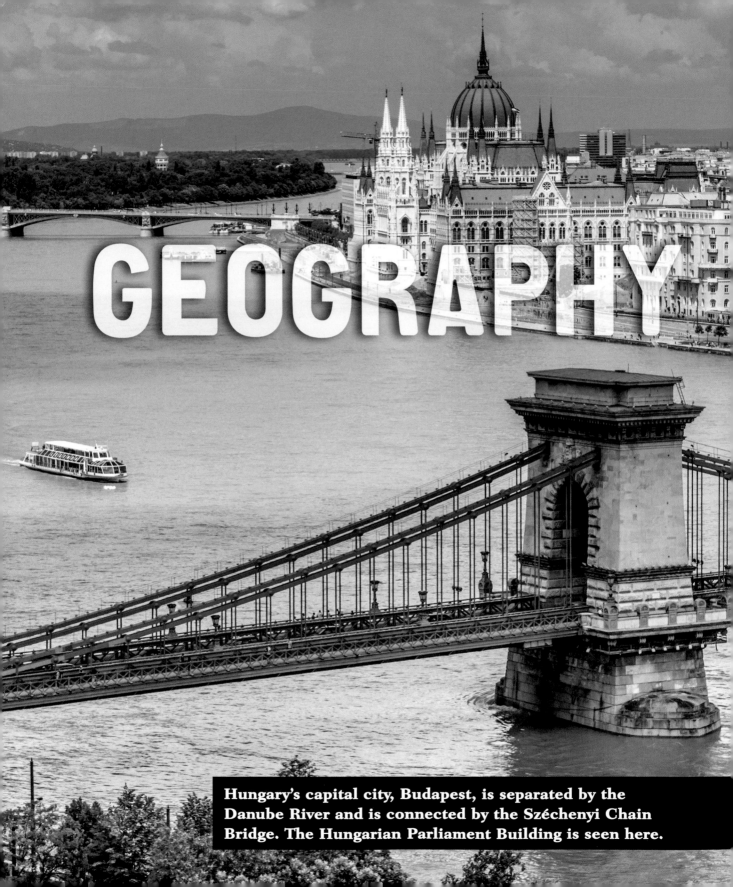

GEOGRAPHY

Hungary's capital city, Budapest, is separated by the Danube River and is connected by the Széchenyi Chain Bridge. The Hungarian Parliament Building is seen here.

HUNGARY IS A LANDLOCKED NATION defined by water. The Danube River in the northwest, the Ipel in the north, and the Mur and Drava rivers in the southwest form part of Hungary's borders. In all, its borders are crossed by twenty-four rivers. The Danube flows north-south, right through the center of today's Hungary, and right through its capital city, Budapest. The entire country lies within the Danube's drainage basin.

Many areas along the Danube maintain their rural charm.

An aerial view of Hungary shows the flat lands that have become invaluable to farming.

Hungary wasn't always landlocked. From the Middle Ages until World War I, the kingdom of Hungary extended from the snowy peaks of the Carpathian Mountains to the shores of the Adriatic Sea. However, with the 1920 Treaty of Trianon that concluded the war, Hungary lost over 70 percent of its territory, leaving a small, flat country without a coastline. Although this loss caused the Hungarian people much soul-searching, present-day Hungary—characterized by plains, fields, rivers, and lakes—retains its distinctive charms.

A FLAT COUNTRY

Although Hungary is usually described as an Eastern European country, it is actually located near the geographical center of Europe. Hungarians like to think of themselves as Central European, an integral part of the continent and its culture. The country is 35,919 square miles (93,030 square km) in area, roughly the size of Indiana. It is about 328 miles (528 km) from west

to east and 166 miles (267 km) from north to south. Hungary's neighbors are Austria to the west, Slovakia to the north, Ukraine and Romania to the east, and Serbia, Croatia, and Slovenia (all formerly Yugoslavia) to the south and southwest. Political changes since 1989 may have altered the names and identities of Hungary's neighbors, but they have left its borders intact.

Hungary lies in a geographic formation called the Middle Danube Depression. Dominated by one of Europe's largest plains, about two thirds of the country is almost completely flat and less than 650 feet (198 km) in elevation. Hungary retains some small mountain ranges, but its highest peak, Mount Kekes, is only 3,327 feet (1,014 m) high. Because of this, Hungarians have managed to put more than half of their land area under cultivation—more than twice the European average.

What lies below the earth is also noteworthy. In Hungary the temperature underground increases by one degree every 59 feet (18 m) in depth, one-and-a-half times that of the world average. This thermal activity explains the presence of the numerous mineral springs that have been used for centuries

The Szechenyi Spa in Budapest is one of the many locations that take advantage of the thermal waters found throughout Hungary.

for bathing and therapy. The earth also yields substantial mineral resources: coal, magnesium, uranium, copper, lead, zinc, and large amounts of bauxite, which is used in making aluminum.

CLIMATE

Hungary lies at the intersection of three major climatic zones: the Atlantic Coast climate is mild and oceanic; the Mediterranean climate brings rainy winters and hot, dry summers; and the extreme Asiatic climate blows dry winds in from the Russian steppes. This means that Hungary's climate varies from year to year, as one or another of these influences predominates. Temperatures can range from -4°F to 104°F (-20°C to 40°C), with an annual mean of 50°F (10°C). Average rainfall per year is 26 inches (66 cm), generally higher in the western part of the country, but that is also unpredictable.

Areas along the Danube are susceptible to seasonal flooding, like this park in Budapest.

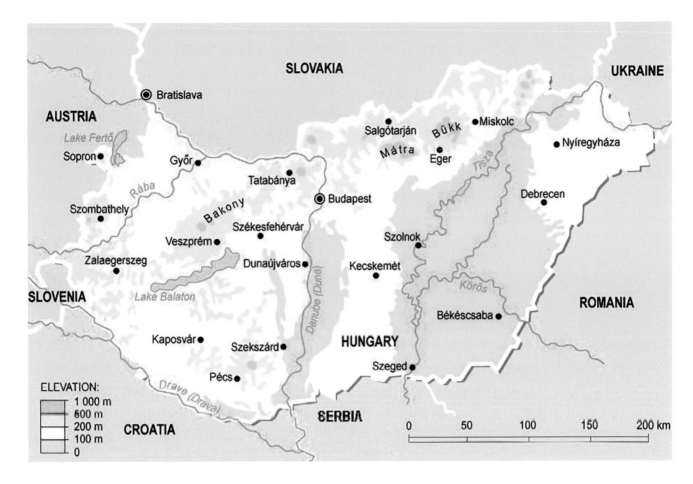

THE GREAT HUNGARIAN PLAIN

To the east of the Danube River stretches the *puszta* (POO-stah), a vast, seemingly empty flatland that forms the heart of Hungary, both physically and spiritually. Like the expanses of the American Midwest, beneath the emptiness lie both wealth and character. When the original Magyar tribes swept into the Hungarian Basin in the ninth century, they found this area of wild grassland ideal for shepherding and horse breeding, their traditional activities. After these semi-nomadic peoples decided to settle down, they planted vineyards and fruit trees, and so began the gradual transformation of barren land into a Central European breadbasket. The driving of huge cattle herds to far-off towns in Italy, Germany, and Austria was gradually

This topographical map of Hungary shows the major rivers and the low-lying lands of the puszta.

replaced by a feudal system of agricultural estates, and the *csikos* (CHEE-kohsh), the Hungarian cowboy, was replaced by landowning nobles and their peasant serfs.

Much of the Great Hungarian Plain (Alfold) is under cultivation, livestock is fenced in, and the only remnants of the csikos are those who perform for foreign tourists. However, parts of the puszta, especially around Hortobagy, retain an elusive, almost mystical charm: subtle coloration, delicate natural balance, sudden and violent changes in weather, the *delibab* (DAY-lee-bahb) or "Hungarian mirage," and man-made landmarks such as the *gemeskut* (GAY-mesh-koot) or *shadoof,* a kind of water-drawing apparatus in the shape of a cross.

RIVERS AND LAKES

Hungary is defined geographically by rivers and lakes. The river systems of the Danube, or *Duna* (DOO-nah) in Hungarian, and the Tisza (TEE-sah) spread out over much of Hungary's territory. Irrigation provided by these two rivers has turned barren grassland into fertile farmland. The western geographical region, between the Danube and the Austrian border, is called *Transdanubia*—"across the Danube." The other two main regions are the Great Plain and the Northern Uplands. The area east of the Tisza has traditionally been referred to as *Tiszántúl* (TEE-sahn-tool), "on the far side of the Tisza." In the past, seasonal flooding by the rivers and their tributaries put much of the surrounding countryside at constant risk of destruction. Flood control measures have now been put in place, and there is less risk of flooding.

Hungary's lakes are dominated by Lake Balaton, the largest lake in Central Europe; the other main lakes are Lake Velence and Lake Ferto (most of which extends into Austria, where it is called *Neusiedler See*). Located about halfway between the Danube and the country's western border, and about one hour from the capital, Lake Balaton is easily accessible to tourists from Western Europe; more than one-third of Hungary's tourist revenue comes from Balaton. Covering a surface area of 230 square miles (596 square km), Lake Balaton is very shallow, averaging only 10 feet (3 m) deep, with a

THE BLUE DANUBE

Many Westerners may think of Austria when they hear about the romantic Danube River—after all, it was the great Austrian composer Johann Strauss II who, in 1866, wrote the famous waltz, "On the Beautiful Blue Danube." It is in Hungary, however, that the river is perhaps most beautiful. The Danube and its eight bridges form the very heart of Budapest, the country's capital. The river cuts the city in two and provides a majestic panorama, which has been declared an international cultural treasure by the United Nations Education and Science Organization (UNESCO).

In the Danube Bend area north of Budapest, where the river takes its great turn to the south, spectacular fortifications, islands, and historic towns can be seen on both banks. The river also provides a major navigational route suitable for ocean-going vessels from Budapest south to Belgrade in Serbia, and then east through Bulgaria and Romania to where it empties into the Black Sea.

From Budapest to the Serbian border, the river takes a slow-moving, gradual course. But this moderation is deceptive: the Danube has often spawned destructive flooding. Ice plugs can develop when the ice begins to break up but is restrained by the still-frozen river downstream. The river then bursts through the "plugs" in a powerful barrage of water and ice.

Such an occurrence wiped out most of the capital (then still three separate cities) in 1838. In 1879, the seasonal second or "green" flood (green because the ice has melted, in contrast to the earlier wintry "white" flood) swelled the Danube to the point where it could not absorb the Tisza's waters, causing a backup on the Tisza that flooded and destroyed the historic city of Szeged. More recently, in June 2013, the river hit a record high of 29 feet (8.91 m) in Budapest, flooding the northern and southern parts of the city. Luckily it did not overflow the city center's flood walls, which are built to a height of 30.5 feet (9.3 m). In 2011 the Danube went to the other extreme during a drought and dwindled to its lowest level in two hundred years, stranding cargo ships from Germany to Bulgaria.

Villages and towns hug the shores of Hungary's huge Lake Balaton.

maximum depth of 36 feet (11 m); the surface freezes completely nearly every winter. The lake has been called a "surrogate sea" for landlocked Hungary, as it moderates temperatures and affects rainfall. In addition to recreational resorts, Balaton's environs harbor unique wetlands, some of which are protected nature reserves for birds. Unfortunately, industrial development, sewage disposal, acid rain, and the draining of the Little Balaton marsh have endangered the Balaton environment.

FLORA AND FAUNA

The undulating lowlands, low hills, grassy plains, rivers, and forests of Hungary are home to some 2,200 plant species and 45,000 animal species.

Twelve percent of Hungary is covered by meadows and pastures, and 18.7 percent is covered by forests (mainly deciduous). Due to the fertility of its soil, about two-thirds of Hungary is used for agriculture, and the remaining 15 percent serves for infrastructure, mining, industrial, military, and domestic use. As a result, native plant cover is rare. A few remaining natural sites include Lake Balata in Somogy, the marshlands of the Nyirseg region, and the chestnut forests of Koszeg. Mixed beech, evergreen, oak, and, less often, pine forests cover the slopes, while acacia groves can be spotted on the Great Plain and western lowlands. Almond, medlar, and fig trees also grow in some places.

Large numbers of deer, wild boar, elk, and fox live in Hungary's forests. Hungary's wild boar is unusual. It is born brown in color with light stripes, but as it grows older, the stripes disappear and the whole coat becomes a uniform dark brown or black. Rabbits, partridge, quail, wild duck, and pheasant can be found in the lower regions.

Baby wild boars, with their unique stripes, stay close to mom in the forests of Hungary.

Hungary's diverse habitats make it one of the best places to bird-watch in Europe. The great bustard, aquatic warbler, corncrake, ferruginous duck, and imperial eagle are just some of the globally threatened species that can be spotted in their natural habitat in Hungary. Large osprey nesting sites also can be seen along the Danube and Drava rivers. Hungary's rivers are also teeming with fish. The native carp, catfish, pike, bream, bullhead, pike-perch, and trout are some examples.

CAPITAL, TOWNS, AND VILLAGES

Early visitors to Hungary described a vast, Asiatic swampland with huge villages. With the development of agriculture, the system of the *tanya* (TAHN-yah)—a kind of plantation-estate, very isolated and home to the wretchedly poor farmhands who worked there—predominated. What remains to this day is the sharp contrast between urban and rural living, characterized by a romanticizing of the countryside by city dwellers on the one hand, and a suspicion of the city by rural citizens on the other.

Today the Hungarian social landscape is dominated by Budapest (BOO-dah-pesht). Originally it was three cities—Obuda and Buda on the west bank

Almost any list of the world's most beautiful cities will include Budapest. Straddling the Danube, the city offers water views along with stunning architecture. Buda on the west bank is hilly and old, and its streets are narrow and winding; Pest on the east bank is the urban center of the city. The city attracts about 4.3 million tourists each year.

The Millennium Memorial

On the Buda side, the Buda Castle Quarter is a UNESCO World Heritage Site. Also called the Royal Palace, it dates to 1265 and is visible from all parts of the city. Today it houses the Budapest History Museum, the Hungarian National Gallery, and the National Szechenyi Library. On the Pest side of the city, Hero's Square, also a World Heritage Site, features the Millennium Memorial, built in 1900 to commemorate the thousand-year anniversary of the arrival of the Magyar tribes who settled the region. The Hungarian Parliament Building, also in Pest, is the third largest parliament building in the world.

The oldest part of the city, the Obuda ("Old Buda") section, is the site of excavated Roman ruins. They date from the second century CE, when the ancient Roman town of Aquincum existed there.

The Roman ruins in Aquincum

Budapest is famous for its thermal baths and spas, and there are many on both sides of the river. On the Pest side, the Szechenyi Medicinal Baths complex is the largest in Europe, with three outdoor and fifteen indoor pools. Its water is supplied by two thermal springs, at natural temperatures of 165 °F (74 °C) and 171 °F (77 °C) respectively. The waters contain minerals that are thought to help certain illness and medical conditions.

of the Danube and Pest on the east bank. The cities unified as the capital in 1873, becoming the largest city in Hungary. In the 2011 census, it was home to 1.74 million residents, down from its peak in 1989 of 2.1 million people. Every day, another million commuters enter the city to work or shop. This huge metropolis is a legacy of its days as a major city in the Austro-Hungarian Empire. Hungary's second largest city, Debrecen, hardly compares to the sprawling capital. There are seven other cities with populations above one hundred thousand, and 69.5 percent of Hungary's population lives in urban areas. Smaller towns, villages, and industrial centers are spread evenly throughout the country.

INTERNET LINKS

www.buzzfeed.com/michaellewis/10-must-visit-places-in-hungary-m8ew
"The 17 Most Amazing Places To Visit In Hungary" is a photo section of interesting places in Hungary.

www.icpdr.org/main/danube-basin/hungary
The International Commission for the Protection of the Danube River has an informative section on Hungary.

www.aviewoncities.com/maps/budapest.htm
An interactive map of Budapest shows the location of many of its attractions.

www.buzzfeed.com/anitabadejo/reasons-budapest-is-the-most-beautiful-city-in-europe#.hi5LoXWdW
"29 Places That Prove Budapest Is the Most Stunning City In Europe" offers superb photos and information.

visitbudapest.travel
This travel site has lots of information and photos.

HISTORY

LONG BEFORE THERE WAS HUNGARY, there was the great Carpathian Basin—sometimes called the Pannonian Basin or Plain—a vast area of flatlands in East-Central Europe, ringed by mountains. To the east lie the Carpathian Mountains that give this geographic area its name. Many centuries ago, these lands were home to various successive nomadic and conquering peoples—Celts, Romans, and Germanic tribes. During its occupation by the Roman Empire, from 20 to 107 CE, the lands made up the province of Pannonia.

The story of Hungary begins when the Magyar tribes of western Asia crossed the Carpathians and settled in the lowlands.

THE GREAT MIGRATION

In 895—896 CE the original seven Magyar (ethnic Hungarian) tribes, led by Prince Árpád, crossed the rugged Carpathian passes into the Carpathian Basin, ending a migration that began in the Ural Mountains and crossed the Asian steppes. The land the Magyars found was once settled by Celtic, Germanic, and Turkic tribes, and was under Roman rule from 14 BCE to 430 CE. By the time the Magyars arrived, the land was

The English name *Hungary* grew out of the Latin terms *Ungri* and *Ungari*, which medieval historians used to describe that region of Central Europe. The Latin names, in turn, probably grew out of the Byzantine Greek *Oungroi*, which evolved from the Bulgar-Turkic term *On-Ogue*, meaning "the ten tribes of the Ogurs."

populated mainly by Slavic tribes; who were soon conquered and enslaved. The Magyars then continued to raid far and wide, gathering booty and slaves. Their success was partly due to their use of metal stirrups and framed saddles that allowed them to stand and shoot their arrows in any direction while riding at full speed. In 955, after a crushing defeat at the hands of German king Otto I, they ceased to venture outside the Danube Basin area.

THE FIRST HUNGARIAN STATE

After their defeat, the Magyars looked around for a favorable alliance. There was a growing rivalry between the Eastern Orthodox Church, based in Constantinople (previously the ancient Greek city of Byzantium, and today's Istanbul, Turkey)—and the Roman Catholic Church, based in Rome. Hungary's leader, Geza, chose to support Rome. With the crowning of his son Vajk as King Istvan (Stephen) by the Pope on Christmas Day of the year 1000, Hungary aligned itself firmly with Western culture, and accepted the Roman Catholic religion. The Hungarian state came into existence.

King Stephen I, the "first European among Hungarians," immediately set about converting his subjects, by force if necessary. His strong hand created a uniform state with an advanced legal code, and the many foreigners he brought into the country created the basis for a multiethnic society. He was made a saint after his death, and despite a messy succession struggle, the Hungarian Kingdom was solidly grounded for the next five centuries.

A statue of Prince Arpad adorns Heroes' Square in Budapest.

THE GOLDEN AGE

Despite bloody struggles for the crown, the country continued to prosper. It benefited from its location astride East—West trade routes, which encouraged the immigration of skilled and enterprising foreign settlers, strengthening the multiethnic nature of the population.

Hungary's progress was abruptly halted by the devastating invasion of the Mongols, led by Batu Khan, in 1241. King Bela IV fled to the coast, and more than half of the population—about one million people—was exterminated or deported as slaves. However, the invaders retreated as suddenly as they had come, and the country was slowly reconstructed, eventually surpassing its former prosperity. King Bela ordered the construction of strong stone castles to defend the country from more invasions.

The Arpad dynasty died out in 1301. Charles Robert of the European noble dynasty the House of Anjou became king of Hungary in 1308, ushering in a Golden Age of peace and prosperity. He reasserted his kingly power over the landowning nobles, increased trade, and developed agriculture and mining—Hungary at that time produced one-third of Europe's gold. He also introduced a stable Hungarian currency—the gold *forint*. His successor Louis the Great expanded the territory, taking over the Dalmatia Coast region on the Adriatic Sea. He fought successfully against the Ottomans and founded the first Hungarian university. By the end of the fourteenth century, the Kingdom of

A Hungarian honor guard rides past the Parliament Building in Budapest during a national celebration

Hungary stretched from Transylvania in the east to the Adriatic in the west. It contained forty-nine cities, more than five hundred towns, and twenty-one thousand villages, with a population of some three million.

Matthias Corvinus Hunyadi reigned from 1458—1490, bringing the full flower of the Italian Renaissance to the country. He invited great thinkers from Florence to share their knowledge, supported Hungarian literature, and built up a library, called the *Corvina*, to rival the greatest of Europe. It contained about three thousand bound, handwritten books, called codices, or *corvinae*, including the works of many classical Greek and Latin authors. These books reflected the state of the arts and knowledge at the time, on a broad array of topics. His reign brought economic prosperity, but he raised taxes to foster artistic growth and to form Hungary's first permanent professional military, called the Black Army. His 1486 Code of Laws put Hungary at the forefront of European legal progress, and earned him the epithet "Matthias the Just."

THE PEASANT REVOLUTION

In 1514, following a papal call to organize a crusade against the Turks, an army was recruited from among Hungary's peasants, who joined up in great numbers, in part because of religious fervor, but even more to escape their cruel lot on the landlords' estates. The landlords, needing their labor—the call coincided with harvest time—and fearing that the army would turn against them, began using force to prevent their serfs from joining. This in turn aroused the peasants even more against their masters. Led by a Transylvanian lower nobleman named Gyorgy Dozsa, they declared a "crusade" against the "wicked nobility" and began destroying the large estates.

The nobles raised an army of their own and, after four months, defeated Dozsa's large but ragged forces. Dozsa, the "peasant king," was forced to sit on a white-hot iron throne with a glowing crown and scepter, and his starved followers were forced to eat his charred flesh before being killed in turn—a kind of violent retribution characteristic of Hungarian history. The nobles' revenge against the peasants took some seventy thousand lives. As if this were not enough, the nobles passed legislation equating the Hungarian nation with only the free noble class, tying the peasantry to the land and depriving them of any rights. The sharp alienation of the peasantry from the ruling elite remained, to some degree, until recent times. Dozsa was glorified by the post—World War II Communist rulers, with statues in his honor and streets named after him in towns across Hungary.

OTTOMAN AND HABSBURG OCCUPATION

In the middle of the fourteenth century, the Ottoman Turks started attacking the Balkan states. The Turks conquered Hungary in 1526 when the army of Sultan Suleiman I killed King Louis II. The Turks took control of most of central Hungary, including the Great Plain and some of Transdanubia (the part of Hungary that lies on the western side of the Danube); the rest of Transdanubia in the west and the northern Carpathian area was controlled by the Habsburgs of Austria. Only Transylvania in the east was granted some independence as a principality under Ottoman rule.

The Battle Monument in Mohács commemorates a battle in 1526, when European armies were defeated by the Ottoman Empire.

A 1724 portrait of Ferenc Rakoczi II

The Ottomans savagely exploited the land and enslaved the people. The Habsburgs were hardly less cruel; discriminatory tariffs and the preservation of a feudal landholding system kept Hungary poor and backward, and maintained it as a source of cheap raw materials for the Habsburgs' growing empire. Constant war between the two powers on Hungarian soil also left the country devastated.

Transylvania, a historic region in the Hungarian Kingdom's easternmost section, became the symbol of the survival of the Hungarian spirit and the preservation of its culture. Many Transylvanian princes struggled for the reunification and liberation of Hungary.

The seventeenth century was filled with Hungarian independence struggles. The most successful was by the *Kuruc* (KOO-roots), a group of armed rebels that aimed to end Habsburg control of Hungary. The Kuruc army, which took on the character of a peasant rebellion as well as national liberation, succeeded in occupying Upper Hungary and part of Austria. Subsequently, under the hero Ferenc Rakoczi II, the army posed a serious threat to the Habsburg court before being forced to surrender in 1711.

After the failure of the Rakoczi Rebellion, Hungary reconciled itself to Habsburg rule. Empress Maria Theresa developed the devastated country, building roads and schools and draining the marshlands. She did not, however, support industry, introduce land reform, or allow the reunification of Transylvania with Hungary proper. She centralized the government and favored Latin over Hungarian as the language of governance. The situation of the peasantry, oppressed by both imperial rule and Hungarian landlords, worsened with the growing demand for grain in Western Europe. When Maria Theresa's successor, Joseph II, tried to initiate rational economic and governmental reforms in the guise of an "enlightened absolutism," the Hungarian nobles resisted. Joseph relented, and instead of modernization sought the greatest economic benefit for the empire from taxing the feudal estate system.

THE PROBLEM OF TRANSYLVANIA

Transylvania, a region in the eastern Carpathian Basin, has switched hands numerous times in its history, controlled by different peoples and countries over the centuries. Much of the time, it was part of the Hungarian Kingdom, and sometimes not. There are supposedly two histories of Transylvania, the Hungarian and the Romanian versions, each country claims the territory was first settled by its own people. Magyars allegedly settled the region in the ninth century, when they arrived in the basin; alternately Romanian people from Wallachia came down from the mountains which form the southern border of Transylvania.

Whoever came first, they were joined by Germanic settlers known as Saxons, who also stayed in the region. The ruling nobility was mainly made up of Europeans, including Magyars. They received the support of the Austrian Habsburg Empire, centered in Vienna. Despite a revolt by Romanian peasants in 1784–1785, Hungarian influence was reinforced in the years that followed. During the nineteenth century, the Kingdom of Hungary began a policy of Magyarization, the implementation of Hungarian culture in the region, with the intention of making it the dominant culture. Hungarian became the official language.

When Romania entered World War I in 1916, on the side of the Allies fighting against the Austro-Hungarian Empire, it attacked Hungarian forces in Transylvania.

After the war, the Austro-Hungarian Empire collapsed, and Romania claimed (or reclaimed) Transylvania. During World War II (1939–1945), a part of Transylvania was given back to Hungary by Adolf Hitler in the Second Vienna Award of 1940. After the war ended with the victory of the Allies, Transylvania was once again fully reunited with Romania in 1947, where it remains today.

After centuries of shifting rule, with its conflicting loyalties, opposition, and repression, relations between the Transylvanian ethnic Romanian majority and the Hungarian minority remain strained. Both Romania and Hungary still claim Transylvania as their own territory.

GROWTH OF NATIONAL CONSCIOUSNESS

In the nineteenth century nationalism spread across Europe. In Hungary, the national renaissance began with an exploration of the native Magyar contributions to Hungarian history. A class of intellectuals, drawn from the lower and middle nobility, favored the use of Hungarian over Latin and German. They were concerned about the social and economic development of the nation. By the time of the "First Reform Generation" of the 1830s, the rich landowners had begun to realize that Hungary's increasing backwardness and poverty were harming them too, and that reform was necessary for modernization.

Count Istvan Szechenyi

The two most prominent Hungarian statesmen of the nineteenth century, Count Istvan Szechenyi and Lajos Kossuth, both now celebrated as national heroes, are a study in contrasts. Szechenyi was a practical, realistic liberal reformer who dedicated himself to building and strengthening the country; he believed steady pressure on the government by an educated people was the most effective way to achieve reform. Kossuth was a national revolutionary with a romantic vision; he wanted to unleash the masses against the enemies of the nation. Szechenyi had grave misgivings about Kossuth's radical course, but it was Kossuth's Freedom Struggle of 1848 that led to a short-lived Hungarian liberation.

REVOLUTION AND COMPROMISE

On March 15, 1848, the poet Sandor Petofi recited a poem called "National Song" to a group of young men in a Pest-Buda (the capital's old name) café, setting off the Hungarian national revolution. The same day, Kossuth arrived in Vienna to meet with the emperor; he was granted his radical reforms, and a virtually independent Hungarian government was installed.

However, by the end of the year, the revolutionary tide had ebbed, and the Austrian rulers were ready to take their revenge. The powerful imperial army descended on Pest-Buda and smothered the new state. Kossuth and his followers retreated to eastern Hungary, and in a stunning turnaround, the Hungarian army drove out the Austrians from their capital. But at this point geopolitics intervened: the young Habsburg Emperor Franz Joseph I urgently requested assistance from Czar Nicholas of Russia, and the huge Russian army marched in to put an end to the revolution. Hungary was subjected to a merciless and humiliating occupation. Kossuth fled the country and spent the rest of his long life in exile, agitating for Hungarian independence. Count Szechenyi, on the other hand, ended up in a mental asylum in Austria, where he committed suicide some years later.

By the 1860s, Austria's hold on Hungary had been weakened by passive resistance on the part of the Hungarians, tensions among other nationalities within the empire, and a weakening international position. The Hungarian statesman Ferenc Deak, a brilliant constitutionalist and indefatigable negotiator, pressed Emperor Franz Joseph for concessions. After the Prussian army defeated the Austrians in 1866, the emperor realized that, more than anything, he needed stability and peace at home, and the next year he agreed to the Compromise of 1867. The Compromise transformed the Habsburg Empire into an Austro-Hungarian monarchy—a dualistic state granting Hungary full sovereignty in conducting its internal affairs.

This painting portrays the coronation of Emperor Franz Joseph and Empress Elizabeth of Austria as King and Queen of Hungary in 1867.

THE POET-LIBERATOR

Sandor Petofi was barely twenty-five years old when he inspired the March 15 uprising in Budapest. Petofi joined the national army and was killed in battle against the invading Russians on July 31, 1849. (Other reports claimed he died a prisoner-of-war in Siberia.) He had a premonition of his fate, expressed in his poem "One Thought Torments Me," which includes the lines: "Let me die on that battlefield. Let my young blood flow there from my heart … And above my corpse wheezing horses will trot off to the well-deserved victory, leaving me trampled to death."

Petofi's poetry was lyrical and mixed romantic love with nationalistic feelings. Every young Hungarian knows his poem "Freedom, Love" by heart. Petofi remains for many Hungarians a national hero and martyr.

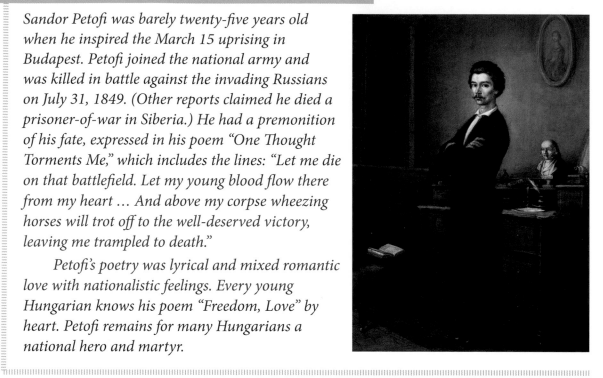

The Austro-Hungarian monarchy, with its sole ruler who was both King of Hungary and Emperor of Austria, lasted until the outbreak of World War I. Hungarian culture flourished, and a relatively liberal and democratic political order was established. Jews and other minorities were invited to adopt the Magyar language and culture, and thus be considered fully Hungarian and equal citizens. This "generous" gesture was in effect forcible assimilation, and the minorities as a whole were excluded from political power. In addition, the nobles retained their privileged position, and the peasant masses remained in squalor and misery. The issues were largely ignored in the whirl of progress: however, in 1896, the 1,000-year anniversary of the Magyar tribes' migration was celebrated with an exposition and the inauguration of the first subway line on the European continent, and the "Second Reform Generation" developed plans to modernize the economic and political system.

WORLD WAR I

The outbreak of World War I put an abrupt end to the Austro-Hungarian monarchy's prosperity. Hungary entered the war on the side of the Central Powers (Germany, the Austrian-Hungarian Empire, the Ottoman Empire, and Bulgaria) and suffered a crushing defeat at the hands of the Allies.

In the chaos of wartime, movements for radical social and political change arose. At the end of the war, a bourgeois (middle-class) democratic revolution swept Count Mihaly Karolyi into power in Budapest. However, he resigned soon after, and a Bolshevik regime headed by Bela Kun took over in March 1919. In the confusion, Czech, Romanian, and Serbian troops occupied large parts of Hungary, with the Romanians capturing Budapest in August. Admiral Miklos Horthy's counter-revolutionary army finally restored order after the Romanians left in November. Horthy was appointed regent in place of a king in 1920.

Later in 1920, the Treaty of Trianon deprived Hungary of two-thirds of its territory and more than 60 percent of its population. American

The Hungarian delegation arrives at the Trianon peace negotiations in 1920.

President Woodrow Wilson's declaration of the self-determination of nations guaranteed the right of Czechs, Slovaks, Romanians, Serbs, and Croats to be joined with their new countries, but Hungarians felt that they were treated unfairly, since about one-third of Magyars along Hungary's borders were left in neighboring Czechoslovakia, Romania, and Yugoslavia for political or strategic reasons.

Soviet troops fight during the Battle of Budapest in 1945.

INTERWAR HUNGARY AND WORLD WAR II

In the early 1930s, young writers and students of the populist movement went to the countryside to investigate the wretched lifestyle of the peasants. They celebrated the peasants as the suffering "true Magyars" and called for radical land reform and social justice. In the capital, writers agitated for a free press, a democratic government, and workers' rights. At the same time, growing anti-Semitic feelings (hatred of Jews) fed a growing fascist movement—a nationalist, authoritarian, political movement that opposed "outsiders."

The Horthy regime resisted the pressures from both left and right. In events leading up to the start of World War II in 1939, Hungary turned to Germany for help in regaining its lost territories.

Germany annexed Austria on March 12, 1938, and in September of that year, Nazi leader Adolf Hitler got the other European powers to agree to his plan to annex part of Czechoslovakia. Hungary was rewarded for its support with the gift of most of the area it had lost to Czechoslovakia eighteen years earlier. Hitler brought about the return of Transylvania to Hungary in 1940, and the territories in Yugoslavia in 1941. In return, Hungary sent troops to fight with the Axis. Meanwhile, Hungary's leaders, realizing that Germany was losing the war, opened secret negotiations with the Allies. Hitler found out, and the German army occupied Hungary in March 1944 and installed the fascist Arrow Cross party into power. The Soviets invaded later that year and, after a destructive battle for Budapest, liberated Hungary on April 4, 1945.

JEWS IN HUNGARY

Jews were in Hungary before the Hungarians were. There were Jewish settlements in the Carpathian Basin a good 600 years before the arrival of the Magyars. Nevertheless, Jews were always a minority in this land, and life was rarely easy. Over the centuries, various forms of discrimination, oppression, expulsion, and outright massacre were brought to bear against the Jewish population. The reigns of Matthias Corvinus (1458–1490), the Ottoman Empire regime (1541–1699), and the Habsburg Emperor Joseph II (1765–1790), a reformer who advocated religious tolerance, were some of the few periods of relative political benevolence toward the Jews.

The rise of Nazism in the twentieth century brought unprecedented disaster for the Jews of Europe. In 1938, under Nazi pressure, Hungary passed several stringent anti-Semitic laws that prohibited Jews from marrying non-Jews and put other restrictions on Jewish participation in social and economic life.

After the Nazis invaded Hungary in 1944, they ordered the deportation of the "Jewish vermin." Within a few months, Hungarian police led by fanatical Arrow Cross militants packed hundreds of thousands of Jews—and Roma (gypsies) too—into freight cars and sent them to their deaths at Auschwitz and other Nazi camps.

The Jews of Budapest, who had played a prominent role in the city's social, economic, and cultural life, were to be deported last, but by then the Soviet army was already nearing the capital. The heroic efforts of Raoul Wallenberg, a Swedish diplomat, saved thousands of Jews: he gave them false identity papers and provided them with Swedish protection. Wallenberg, ironically, was later arrested by Soviet officers and disappeared in a Siberian prison camp. Thus, most of the Jews of Budapest—about 100,000—were spared, and the Jewish community continues to be important in the city's, and Hungary's, life today.

Empty shoes, cast from actual victims' shoes, make up the "Shoes on the Danube Bank" monument in Budapest. It commemorates the Jews killed by fascist Arrow Cross militiamen in Budapest during World War II.

BETWEEN WAR AND COMMUNISM

At the end of the war, Hungary once again found itself on the losing side, this time occupied by the victorious Soviet army. A provisional government that heavily favored the Communists and was supported by the Soviets was set up in December 1944, although the Populists and other parties were also included.

In the November 1945 election, the Smallholders Party, representing the interests of small farmers and the middle class, won 57 percent of the vote, and the Communist Party received only 17 percent. The new government began rebuilding the country—nationalizing industries, mines, plants, and banks, as well as collectivizing agriculture. Although Soviet forces still occupied the country and seized whole factories, mines, and other economic resources as "war reparations," Hungarians believed that they could maintain their independence and a democratic system.

When tensions between the United States and the Soviet Union grew into the Cold War, the Soviets became determined to fully control the Eastern European political systems. Hungary's Communist leaders, eager for power, used Soviet pressure to squeeze out the other parties. These tactics included accusing opponents of being American spies and conspiring against Hungary. The leaders of the other parties, such as Prime Minister Ferenc Nagy of the Smallholders, were arrested or fled the country, and by 1948, the Communist Party was in full control.

FROM COMMUNISM TO INDEPENDENCE

Hungary's Communist authorities, led by Matyas Rakosi, forced a Stalinist system on Hungary. They outlawed all associations and organizations they could not control. They introduced Soviet-style central planning and the production of consumer goods was neglected in favor of heavy industries. The population was terrorized, and prisons and labor camps were filled with opponents and those whose family background was "suspicious."

Soviet leader Joseph Stalin's death in 1953 created an atmosphere of reform and strict centralized control was relaxed. Mass anti-Soviet demonstrations in Poland in the first half of 1956 encouraged a similar demonstration by students in Budapest on October 23 of that year. The rebellion soon spread throughout the country, and workers' councils took over the factories. Imre Nagy, a Communist who believed in a more humane "Hungarian socialism," became prime minister and urged the rebel bands to lay down their arms, while trying to convince the Soviets that the situation could be resolved. Instead, the Soviet army invaded Hungary on

János Kádár speaks to the Hungarian Parliament in 1980.

November 4, crushing the rebellion and killing some 30,000 in Budapest alone. The Soviets placed János Kádár in power in return for his promise to do their bidding. Soviet reprisals included prison for more than 25,000 and the execution of 229, including Imre Nagy. Approximately 200,000 refugees left the country. Once again, Hungary lay devastated.

But Kádár was smart enough to know that the Stalinist era of total control of the people was over. He gave in to some of the demands of the revolutionaries, such as ending the drive to collectivize agriculture, while condemning the uprising itself as a "counter-revolution" led by "fascists and spies." While remaining a loyal subject of the Soviet Union, Kádár was able to liberalize the economic system in Hungary, provide people with a better standard of living and privileges such as owning a car or a vacation house and the right to travel to the West (unheard of in the other Communist countries), and gain some autonomy for his country.

By the 1980s, Hungary appeared very liberal—it was known as the "happiest barracks in the Communist concentration camp." But much of the industrial reform was artificially constructed, unemployment concealed by three workers doing one man's job, the standard of living supported by money borrowed from abroad, and the government shortsighted and corrupt.

After Soviet leader Mikhail Gorbachev began the changes in the Soviet system known as *glasnost* ("transparency" or "openness") and *perestroika* ("restructuring"), the leaders of the Eastern European countries, including Hungary, found it harder to resist similar changes themselves.

Kádár was removed from power, and the new government agreed to enter negotiations with the opposition groups, which resulted in an agreement to hold free, multiparty elections in early 1990 and to move to a market economy and a parliamentary democracy. In 1989 Hungary also allowed thousands of refugees from East Germany to pass unhindered across its border into Austria, a decision that played a major role in the fall of the Berlin Wall and the "Iron Curtain."

Hungary was proclaimed an independent republic on October 23, 1989. All governments since 1990 have moved toward full Euro-Atlantic integration: Hungary joined the North Atlantic Treaty Organization (NATO) in 1999 and became a member of the European Union (EU) in 2004. NATO is a military alliance of member governments committed to mutual and collective defense. Its members include Canada, the United States, and many, but not all, nations of Western and Central Europe. The European Union is a political and economic coalition of European member states (in 2015, there are twenty-eight) that adhere to certain standards of law and function as a single market.

TWENTY-FIRST CENTURY

Quality of life in Hungary continued to improve until the election of a new government in 2006. The Socialist coalition administration of Prime Minister Ferenc Gyurcsány planned to remove certain subsidies, increase taxes, and greatly restructure the economy with the goal of achieving sustainable economic growth. The public balked and people held protests and Gyurcsány eventually resigned in 2009. The global financial crisis of 2008 caused further budget restraints and hardship.

Since then the conservative Fidesz party has taken power through two consecutive Parliamentary electoral wins in 2010 and 2014. Supported by the apparent public mandate expressed by sweeping victories, the party instituted many new laws and rewrote the Hungarian Constitution. Critics say the new constitution gives too much power to the ruling party and eliminates the checks and balances necessary to a democratic government. Indeed, concerned observers in Europe and beyond sense a strategic shift to authoritarianism.

In July 2014, Hungarian Premier Viktor Orbán said, "The wind is blowing from the East," expressing his opinion that the Russian authoritarian state was an attractive alternative to Western-style democracy.

Hungarian prime minister Viktor Orbán holds a press conference in Budapest in 2010.

INTERNET LINKS

news.bbc.co.uk/2/hi/europe/country_profiles/1054642.stm
BBC News: Hungary timeline lays out a coherent chronology of key events.

www.jewishvirtuallibrary.org/jsource/vjw/Hungary.html
Jewish Virtual Library has an excellent overview of the history of Jews in Hungary.

www.pbs.org/wgbh/amex/holocaust/peopleevents/pandeAMEX100.html
The *American Experience*, "America and the Holocaust" site has an interesting listing for Raul Wallenberg and the role he played in Hungary.

www.slate.com/articles/news_and_politics/moment/2014/10/viktor_orban_s_authoritarian_rule_the_hungarian_prime_minister_is_destroying.html
"Hungary at the Turning Point," an article on *Slate*, is an informative look at the recent political situation in Hungary.

GOVERNMENT

Gabor Vona, center, leader of the Jobbik Party, casts his ballot with his wife and son in the 2014 election.

3

AN OLD SAYING GOES THAT IF YOU have three Hungarians in a room, they will form four political parties. The joke pokes fun at how opinionated Hungarians supposedly are, but it also—perhaps inadvertently—comments on the political freedom that Hungarians now enjoy.

Hungary has changed its political system from one where a single party, the Hungarian Socialist Workers' Party, controlled every aspect of government to one in which different political parties, with different ideas and representing different constituencies, freely compete for the votes of citizens.

The road to democracy has not been easy. After more than forty years of repressive Communist rule, the people left behind old habits and mindsets—blind obedience to leaders and belief in official lies. Still, Hungary's big step from communism to a multiparty democracy and the private ownership of property has occurred at an incredible pace, which in itself was bound to cause some upheaval.

Hungary's government is a parliamentary democracy made up of three branches: the executive, the legislative, and the judiciary. The executive branch is made up of the president, the prime minister, and the Cabinet of Ministers; the legislative, or law-making, branch is the parliament; and the judicial branch is the court system. The foundation of Hungarian law is the Fundamental Law, also called the Constitution.

In October 2014, the Hungarian government planned to tax Internet use, saying it was an extension of the telephone tax, since much communication had moved online. But tens of thousands of Hungarians took to the streets of Budapest in protest and the government backed off.

THE CONSTITUTION

In 2013, Hungarian protesters take to the streets of Budapest to demonstrate against the new national Constitution.

When the conservative Fidesz Party won the 2010 Parliamentary elections, thereby making Viktor Orbán the prime minister, the new government undertook some radical changes. Among them was the rewriting of the country's constitution, reportedly without input from other political parties. In 2011, the Hungarian Parliament adopted the new Constitution. It went into effect in 2012, completely preempting the previous one .

The official reason for the change, as stated on the government's website, is that the previous constitution, written in 1949, was modeled on the 1936 Soviet Constitution. Although the document was amended several times over the years, and radical changes were made to it in 1989, after the fall of Communism, it was still essentially the same outdated constitution.

"By adopting the new Fundamental Law," the government website explains, "Hungary also closed the door on the past in a symbolical sense, since our country was the last one among the states of the former communist bloc to replace its Soviet model-based constitution. The new Constitution opened a new chapter in the history of the country. The former Fundamental Law, issued in 1949, has now been replaced by a Constitution written by Hungary itself, committed to both national and European values."

The new Constitution was criticized, both in Hungary and internationally. The new document, critics charge, reflects and codifies the view of the ruling party and centralizes power. It also injects Christian ideology into the law of a supposedly secular state, and limits certain civil liberties. For example, the new Fundamental Law states that marriage is between a man and a woman, which blocks any possibility of legalized same-sex marriage in Hungary. In 2013, the Constitution was amended, to the further consternation of critics—including the European Union, the US State Department, and many other individuals, governments, and organizations.

THE EXECUTIVE BRANCH

PRESIDENT Hungary's president is the head of state, and is elected to a five-year term. According to the Constitution, the president "embodies the nation's unity and safeguards the democratic operation of state organization." He or she is also the Commander in Chief of the Hungarian Armed Forces; represents the nation in international affairs; and, working with the prime minister, appoints various ministers and judges. Working with the parliament, the president can introduce laws and national referenda. In addition, if deemed necessary, the president can send any laws passed by National Assembly to the Constitutional Court for review.

Hungarian president Janos Ader in 2013

THE PRIME MINISTER The prime minister is the head of government, and is the most powerful person in Hungarian politics. He or she is elected by the National Assembly, on the recommendation of the president, and is traditionally the leader of the political party with the most seats in parliament. The prime minister serves a five-year term and is eligible for a second consecutive term. He or she choses the Cabinet, chairs its meetings, and determines the direction of government policy.

THE LEGISLATURE

Hungary's parliament, the "National Assembly," is a unicameral (one chamber) lawmaking body. It consists of 199 members of parliament (MPs), who are elected to four-year terms in a single round of voting. Prior to the adoption of the new constitution in 2012, there were 386 MPs, who were elected after two rounds of voting. The assembly meets in the House of Parliament in Budapest.

In December 2011, the National Assembly enacted a new law on the election of MPs. It was applied for the first time during the general election of April 2014. That spring, nearly eight million citizens elected 199 MPs to four-

year terms, voting directly by secret ballot based on universal and equal suffrage. The voting age in Hungary is eighteen, or sixteen if the person is married.

For the first time, citizens of a particular nationality in Hungary were able to elect a nationality representative. Thirteen Hungarian nationalities, each with its own self-governing body, nominated candidates on a nationality list. It was also the first time Hungarian citizens living abroad were able to vote.

On June 6, 2014, members of the newly elected Hungarian government take the oath of office during a ceremony in the main hall of the Parliament Building.

THE JUDICIARY

The Curia, or Supreme Judicial Court, is the highest judicial authority in Hungary. It has three departments: criminal, civil, and administrative-labor law, and consists of a president and eight judges. The Curia president is elected from among its members for nine years by the National Assembly on the recommendation of the executive branch; other Curia judges are appointed by the president on the recommendation of the National Council of Justice, a separate fifteen-member administrative body. Judges serve until retirement age.

The Constitutional Court consists of fifteen members. It reviews laws, and can challenge legislation on grounds of it being unconstitutional. Its members are elected by two-thirds vote of the National Assembly and serve twelve-year terms.

There are also subordinate courts: regional courts of appeal; county courts, including the Municipal Court of Budapest; and local courts. In addition, there are several ombudsman positions in Hungary responsible for protecting civil, minority, educational, and ecological rights in non-judicial

matters. They have the authority to issue legally binding decisions in the cases they mediate.

POLITICAL PARTIES

From 1998 until the 2010 elections, Hungary's political parties kept a stable balance, with elections closely matched between Fidesz and the Hungarian Socialist party (MSZP). In 1998, the Fidesz party won the most seats and formed a conservative, right-wing coalition government with Viktor Orbán as the prime minister.

Socialist Ferenc Gyurcsány was the prime minister from 2004—2009. Following his time in office, the leftist parties lost their strength and popularity. Meanwhile, the conservative Fidesz party gained strength, and the far-right, nationalist Jobbik party, known for its anti-Semitism and anti-Roma bigotry, grew in popularity.

In 2010, the Fidesz party scored an overwhelming victory at the polls, sweeping in a new, right-leaning government. Viktor Orbán resumed the position of prime minister, and in 2014, his party won big again, so he remained in office. In that same election, the Jobbik party took 20 percent of

TOO MANY LIES OR TOO MUCH TRUTH?

In 2006, Prime Minister Ferenc Gyurcsány gave a speech to members of his party, the MSZP. The speech was supposed to be confidential but, unknown to the prime minister, it was taped and broadcast several months later on the radio. In the speech, Gyurcsány used a good deal of obscene and derogatory language, even in describing the country. He also admitted to lying in order to win the election. He said the country was broken, that he didn't know how to fix it, and that he had made mistakes. Some of his controversial remarks from that speech include the following quotes:*

- "No European country has done something as boneheaded as we have. Obviously, we lied throughout the last year-and-a-half, two years."

- "And meanwhile, by the way, we've done nothing for four years. Nothing."

- "I almost perished because I had to pretend for eighteen months that we were governing. Instead, we lied morning, night and evening."

- "There will be protests, there will be. It is allowed to protest in front of the Parliament … Sooner or later they will get bored of it and go home."

Gyurcsány was correct; there were indeed protests. In the days following the broadcast, rioters took to the streets of Budapest and other cities, demanding the resignation of Gyurcsány. Some of the protests were peaceful, but others became violent as the rioters lit cars on fire, shattered windows, and stormed the state television building. About 150 people were hurt. Police used tear gas and water cannon to break up the crowds and calm was restored. Naturally, Hungarians were shocked. Nothing like this had happened in their country since the fall of communism.

For his part, Gyurcsány stood by his remarks, saying his speech was "passionate." He explained that all Hungarian politicians lie, and that it would be impossible to be elected any other way—"The lies are the sins of the whole Hungarian political elite," he said. Essentially, he explained that the country's financial situation was in crisis and no one wanted to admit it. He added, "The real issue in Hungarian politics today is not who lied and when, but who is able to put an end to this, who can face up to the lies and half-truths of the past sixteen years."

*These quotes are taken out of context, though not misrepresented; the text of the speech is available online in English.

the vote and came to represent Orbán's most powerful political rival.

During Orbán's administration, observers noted a significant shift in his political views, away from liberal democracy and toward authoritarianism. In 2014, Orbán made news and rattled European and other Western allies by advocating a form of "illiberal" nationalism. He said the liberal democracies of Europe and the United States were no longer viable and that Russia, China, and Turkey were attractive political models for Hungary.

INTERNET LINKS

www.kormany.hu/en
This is the official website of the Hungarian government, in English.

www.jacobinmag.com/2014/01/hungary-after-communism
Jacobin magazine offers "Hungary After Communism," a very interesting article on the Hungarian government's shift to the right.

www.theguardian.com/world/2006/sep/19/1
The Guardian article "150 injured as Hungarians riot over PM's lies" reports on the aftermath of the broadcast of Ferenc Gyurcsány's controversial speech in 2006.

www.businessweek.com/articles/2015-01-22/power-hungary-viktor-orban-europe-s-new-strongman
Businessweek, "Power Hungary: How Viktor Orban Became Europe's New Strongman" is an in-depth look at Hungary's controversial prime minister.

www.birosag.hu/en/information/hungarian-judicial-system
This is the site of the National Office for the Judiciary in Hungary.

ECONOMY

Fresh vegetables sit on display at a market in Budapest.

4

LIKE ITS NEIGHBORS IN EASTERN Europe, Hungary had a huge task to undertake. After the dissolution of the Soviet Union in 1989 and the subsequent disintegration of communism throughout Eastern Europe, Hungary needed to remake its economy. It would be a swift but painful transition.

"GOULASH COMMUNISM"

The Communists had a grand vision for the peasant country. Their goals were heavy industrialization, the creation of a large working class, and the collectivization of agriculture, turning farmers and farmhands into state employees. Under the principle that the country's resources belong to all the people, the state declared private ownership of land, shops, and factories illegal, and took away all property beyond personal belongings.

In the late 1960s, the regime of János Kádár placed an emphasis on industrial products, but the government, recognizing the low income of its citizens, allowed small private enterprises to be established. This mix of communism with elements of capitalism came to be called "goulash communism." (Goulash is a popular Hungarian dish made of a mixture of unlike ingredients.) These private businesses were mostly shops, and later small restaurants and other food vendors appeared. In agriculture, members of state and collective farms were allowed to rent small plots to cultivate in their spare time. Farmers could keep the profits from

Hungary is the world's second largest producer and top exporter of foie gras, a delicacy made from duck or goose liver. The luxury liver product is controversial, regardless of where it is produced, because it is usually made using force-feeding methods that some people consider inhumane.

A Hungarian man holds up two fresh garlic braids in an outdoor market.

these extra crops. The state, meanwhile, was to concentrate on producing grain and livestock, which were more capital-intensive. Through this two-tiered system, food products became abundant.

As the control of the economy by Party officials and central planning offices decreased, more and more transactions and exchanges took place outside the official economy between private citizens and even between factories, collective farms, and enterprises. This whole network of trading and services became known as the "second economy," as opposed to the official, or "first", economy.

Nevertheless, the economy was in crisis. In 1988 the government instituted Hungary's first value-added and personal income taxes. People were working harder and harder, yet their standard of living was falling.

BUILDING A NEW ECONOMY

After Communism, Hungary had to transition from a one-party, centrally-planned economy to a market economy with a multi-party political system. It was not an easy process, and life did not immediately get better for most people—in fact, in some ways it got worse. The Communist system left Hungarians with an infrastructure that was old, decaying, and substandard. Many apartment complexes, factories, and streets were in disrepair, and equipment in most manufacturing plants was outdated and inefficient.

Systems that had been holding the Hungarian economy together suddenly evaporated. The political and economic collapse of the Soviet Union, which occurred more or less simultaneous to the fall of Communism in Hungary, caused a great loss of financial support to the Eastern Bloc nations—of which Hungary was one. Without money from the Soviet Union propping up its economy, Hungary suddenly had little money for social programs.

This caused great hardship for many people. In addition, Hungary's trading partners, mostly the Eastern Bloc nations, found themselves in similar straits. Hungary's industries were accustomed to having a captive market locally and in the former Socialist countries. As the market for Hungarian goods dried up, the country lost about 70 percent of its export market. Inefficient and unprofitable factories were closed, leaving some eight hundred thousand people out of work. By 1991, economic growth had fallen by 11.9 percent.

Hungary needed to look elsewhere for trading partners. Within a decade, it had shifted much of its trade to the West. In 1995, it joined the Organization for Economic Co-operation and Development (OECD), an economic group of countries committed to democracy and the market economy. In 2004, it became a member of the European Union (EU), thereby cementing its relationship with Western Europe. Today, trade with EU countries and the OECD makes up between 70—80 percent of Hungary's trade. Germany is its single most important trading partner.

A cargo ship passes through Budapest as it transports goods on the Danube River.

Grapes grow in straight lines at a vineyard in Badacsony.

DEBT, AUSTERITY, AND CRISIS

In the 1990s, during Hungary's economic transition, financial imbalances—caused by a high trade deficit, insufficient foreign investment, debt, and a budget gap, among other things—needed to be addressed. The government imposed austerity measures aimed at creating a stable and sustainable financial situation in the country. Such stability would, in turn, bolster investor confidence and lead to increased foreign revenue. The measure did help, but Hungarians hated the changes, including cuts to welfare allowances, childcare benefits, maternity payments, and medications. The austerity plan also eliminated free college tuition and dental services, limited wage increases in the public sector, and raised the retirement age.

In 2006, Prime Minister Ferenc Gyurcsány ran for re-election on a promise of economic "reform without austerity," He won a second term. However, after the elections, the Socialist coalition government unveiled a package of additional austerity measures designed to reduce the budget deficit to 3 percent of GDP by 2008. Aside from incurring voter wrath, the program slowed the country's economy in 2007. And then the global financial crisis of 2008 hit, sending economies worldwide into a nosedive.

In subsequent elections, the Hungarian people chose to take an about-face. They elected the conservative Fidesz Party and Prime Minister Viktor Orbán, whose policies have alarmed many of Hungary's allies. Nevertheless, whether because of, in spite of, or unrelated to Orbán's changes, the Hungarian economy has shown signs of a slow recovery.

An employee works on an automobile motor at an engine manufacturing plant in Szentgotthard, Hungary, in 2014.

SECTORS

The private sector now accounts for more than 80 percent of the Hungarian gross domestic product (GDP). Foreign ownership of and investment in Hungarian firms—to the tune of more than $70 billion—has helped bring in the money needed to get back on track.

AGRICULTURE Hungary's main agricultural products are wheat, corn, sunflower seeds, potatoes, sugar beets, pigs, cattle, poultry, and dairy products. In addition, it has a vital wine industry, which is well known for its *Tokaji*, or Tokay in English, a sweet white wine, and *pálinka*, a fruit brandy. Hungary's vast, flat landscape and continental climate are well suited for agriculture, and about half of its land is under cultivation. It is one of the world's leading producers of paprika, a spice made from peppers, and is the world's second largest producer of foie gras, a delicacy made from duck or goose liver.

INDUSTRY Hungary's main industries are mining, metallurgy, machine and steel production, construction materials, processed foods, textiles,

ATTRACTING TOURISTS

One product that Hungary has ready to sell is Hungary itself. Budapest is well known as a particularly beautiful city on the Danube, full of architectural wonders. The city also boasts four-hundred-year-old Turkish baths, two-thousand-year-old Roman amphitheaters, spectacular museums, the Buda Palace on Castle Hill, and a lively cultural scene. Farther afield, Hungary offers the picturesque Danube Bend north of Budapest and the 48-mile-long (77 km) Lake Balaton, the largest freshwater lake in Europe, where all manner of summer and winter sports take place.

Tourism is a growing Hungarian economic sector. It accounts for about 9 percent of the country's GDP and employs more than 11 percent of the labor force. More than ten million tourists visit Hungary every year, making Hungary the twenty-third most popular tourist destination in the world. Most tourists come from Germany, followed by Austria and Russia. Slovakian and Czech tourists also make up a large and growing number.

The Hungarian Minister for National Economy reported that in 2014–2020, a good portion of EU funding will be channeled into building up the tourism sector.

chemicals (especially plastics and pharmaceuticals), and motor vehicles. The automobile sector, which generates nearly 21 percent of the country's total exports, employs about one hundred thousand people working in more than six hundred companies. General Motors, Magyar Suzuki, Mercedes Benz, and Audi all have factories in Hungary. Electronics and technology are strong industries, employing another two hundred throusand workers between them. There are also about two hundred large processed food producers.

Although Hungary's transition to a market economy has been largely successful, the country still faces economic challenges. The transition left many unskilled laborers out of work. And the growing Roma population, thought to be around five hundred thousand—seven hundred thousand people, make up a disproportionate number of the unskilled, uneducated, and unemployed. According to economic experts, the government needs to figure out how to integrate those people into the workforce, and raise the employment rate overall. It also needs to improve the quality and efficiency of education and healthcare, tackle the problem of corruption in government and business, and overhaul the tax system to make it more business-friendly.

INTERNET LINKS

eugo.gov.hu
This website has information about Hungary's economy, infrastructure, and business environment.

www.mkik.hu/en
The Hungarian Chamber of Commerce and Industry has up-to-date economic news.

www.kormany.hu/en/ministry-for-national-economy
The website of the Hungarian government has a section about the economy, including news stories in English.

ENVIRONMENT

Greenpeace activists protest against the expansion of a nuclear power plant by installing a giant nuclear sign in downtown Budapest.

5

HUNGARY PASSED ITS FIRST "NATURE protection" law in 1910, but through much of the century, the country's environment suffered. The Stalinist-style industrialization during the Communist years damaged Hungary's waters and lands with untreated sewage, chemical fertilizers, and industrial waste. Toxic chemicals and jet fuel left by the Soviet army contaminated the soil, groundwater, rivers, and lakes.

In 1997, Hungary's parliament enacted the first phase of its National Environmental Program to begin a new "green" chapter in the country's history. In order to join the European Union, which it did in 2004, Hungary had to improve its environmental laws and regulations and devote money to clean-up and protection projects. It did so, and its environmental status began to improve.

Now that a legal framework is in place, implementation is Hungary's next challenge. Laws are only as good as their enforcement, after all, and in Hungary, progress has been hampered by budgetary concerns.

WASTE MANAGEMENT

Hungary has made strides on the problem of waste disposal. The government enacted a new waste management law in 2001 and is

In terms of global climate change, Hungary is reportedly one of the most endangered countries in Europe. The global temperature rise affects the entire Carpathian Basin, and especially Hungary, by a factor of 1.4. This means that 1 degree Celsius of global warming would result in a 1.4 degree warming in this region. That could prove disastrous to some of Hungary's animal and plant species.

carrying out plans for the separation and composting of waste. It is also encouraging the introduction of low-waste technologies, the setting up of comprehensive waste treatment systems, increased responsibility on the part of manufacturers, and the reuse of products.

By 2008, the country had decreased the amount of waste it generates, particularly in the areas of industrial and agricultural production. Hazardous waste levels also decreased significantly. However, the amount of municipal solid waste, which is largely household trash, increased. This is explained by a generally higher standard of living. As personal incomes rise, consumption patterns change. In other words, when people have more money, they buy more stuff, and that generates more garbage. On average, a 2 percent increase in wages results in a 1 percent increase in the quantity of waste. (The opposite is also true: in the years of income stagnation or decline, waste generation decreases.) So Hungary's improved economic situation ironically produced a greater environmental challenge.

The EU-mandated Waste Framework Directive aims to recycle 50 percent of household waste by 2020. That's an ambitious goal for Hungary, which comes late to the recycling habit.

Hungarians are learning to sort their waste to decrease the pollution and keep up with the European Union's standards.

AIR POLLUTION

Hungary's air quality generally matches the average in other EU countries. However, there are significant differences between the air in rural areas and larger cities, and some places where air quality is still below an acceptable level.

Hungary has made great progress in the reduction of industrial pollutant emissions, a result of stricter regulations. This has been partially offset, however, by an increase in road transport. Following Hungary's admission to the EU, the country experienced a boom in the volume of its road freight transport. Despite improvements in vehicle technology and fuel quality, the new traffic has become one of the biggest sources of air pollution.

In Budapest, an increase of tourism has brought about a proliferation of tour buses, with accompanying exhaust fumes. Households contribute to the air pollution problem too. Hungarians often burn household and garden waste in a furnace or a back garden. Public education is part of the overall solution for achieving a healthy environment.

Double decker tour buses cause double trouble for pollution rates in Budapest.

WATER POLLUTION

Although Hungary is a landlocked nation, it has abundant water resources. Hungary's lakes, including Lake Balaton, the largest shallow lake in Central Europe, are fully or partially protected by law as wetlands of international importance. The country is also well known for its abundant, world-famous mineral and thermal waters, which are also protected. Its rivers and lakes are highly vulnerable, however, as 96 percent of Hungary's surface water supply comes from neighboring countries. Pollution from those countries can end up in Hungary. The cyanide spill in Romania in 2000 is a good example.

One of Hungary's most serious water pollution issues is the contamination of groundwater with arsenic in the Carpathian Basin. According to a study

THE DIRTY DANUBE

Hungarians say the Duna, *or Danube, is most beautiful as it flows through Hungary. The river is certainly a national treasure—indeed, the Danube Banks in Budapest are a UNESCO World Heritage site. The beauty of the Danube inspired the Austrian composer Johann Strauss to write "On the Beautiful Blue Danube" waltz in 1867, one of the world's best loved waltzes. Today he might call it "The Dirty Danube" and turn it into a dirge. The great river—and its tributaries—have been polluted by oil spills, toxic mine spills, industrial discharge, and bombs.*

The Danube flows through ten countries from Germany to Romania, dumping about 1653.5 tons (1500 tonnes) of waste into the Black Sea each year. It picks up pollutants before it even reaches Hungary. In Germany and Austria, there are dozens of plastic production and processing plants on the river's banks, and plastic pollution is a serious problem which harms wildlife. In the former Soviet bloc nations, including Hungary, Communist regimes built up heavy industry along the waterway with little regard for environment. Today in western Hungary, hazardous waste in the form of toxic sludge pours into the river. Agricultural runoff from farms throughout Europe drains into the river and ends up polluting the Black Sea.

In the river beyond Hungary, the 1990s war in neighboring Serbia contributed to the mess when bombed out chemical and fertilizer factories spilled their toxic brew into the waters. In Romania, in 2000, a wall collapsed at a gold mine in the northwest region of Baia Mare. The calamity released cyanide  *and heavy metals into the river and poisoned drinking water across the Balkans.*

Despite all this, environmentalists say the situation is improving and now that eight Danube countries are part of the European Union, the EU's stiffer regulations and standards should help in the long run.

published in 2011, some five hundred thousand people living in Hungary and Romania were exposed to levels of arsenic in their drinking water that are considered unsafe by the EU. The EU has given Hungary several deadlines by which to comply with the EU Drinking Water Directive, but they have come and gone without success. Government officials on the local level said they didn't have the financial resources to fix the problem.

In 2013, the national government stepped in and took over thirty-three local water projects, stripping the local officials of their authority. These projects will improve water quality for 227 settlements, about half of those affected by the contaminated water. To date, most of the projects are still in the planning phases.

NATIONAL PARKS

About 20 percent of Hungary's original woodland has been seriously damaged, due to aggressive agricultural cultivation and forestry, rapid industrialization in the twentieth century, and environmental pollution. Shrinking natural habitats have led to the disappearance of the European bison, and the beaver, lynx, wolf, and auroch. Some 535 plants, 855 animal species, and all 3,600 caves are now protected. Protected flora include the Great Plain's wild peony, spring adonis, and sage; the forest cyclamen flower found in western Transdanubia, and the meadow anemone found in the Nyírség. Protected birds include the egret, bustard, plover, and avocet. Animals on Hungary's endangered list include the European mink, Bechstein's bat, Eurasian otter, European squirrel, and lesser mole rat. Fortunately, the threat to animal and plant species in Hungary is still not as high as in some Western European countries.

Ten national parks, thirty-eight landscape protection zones, and 160 nature protection areas have been set aside to preserve Hungary's flora and fauna. Hungary's first and most famous national park and Central Europe's largest area of *puszta* ("grassland") is Hortobágy National Park. Under protection since 1972, Hortobágy's total territory is 200,155 acres (81,000 hectares). It was listed as a World Heritage Site in 1999. Hortobágy has three landscapes: floodplain forests and ox-bow lakes, marshes and lakes, and the

The stepped Veil Waterfall in the Szalajka Valley is a popular tourist destination in northern Hungary.

puszta. The Hortobágy Puszta is Hungary's most important semi-nomadic shepherding region and early Magyar domesticated animals—Hungarian gray cattle, the Hungarian *racka* (RAH-tskah) breed of sheep, and Hungarian horses and buffalo—roam freely here. The mirages on the arid puszta have been immortalized in Hungarian myth and legend.

Kiskunság National Park was founded in 1975 and spans an area of nearly 188,000 acres (76,000 hectares) between the Danube and the Tisza rivers. The Bócsa-Bugac sand dunes and puszta form the park's largest and most variable section featuring sandy forests, alkaline grasslands, dunes, salt lakes, marshes, meadows, and fields. Many species of indigenous Hungarian flora and fauna and traditional peasant farming methods and lifestyles still exist here.

More than 90 percent of Bükk National Park is covered by forest. Beneath the limestone Bükk Hills are 500—600 caves, which extend to a total of about 22 miles (35 km). Stone Age tools and fossils of flora dating back to the Ice Age have been discovered in them. This park is famous for its stepped waterfall, with a fall of 56 feet (17 m), along the Szalajka stream. The Aggtelek National Park is also known for its cave system.

Orség National Park in southwest Hungary, opened in 2002, is home to 111 protected species of flora. Many traditional log-wall houses and U-shaped Orség houses are found here, as well as precious deer stocks and the breeding grounds for forty-five species of fish.

Sixty percent of Hungary's birds are found in the Danube-Ipoly National Park in the north. Körös-Maros National Park, in the southwest, is a sanctuary for bustards. The Balaton National Park is a nesting site for about 250 bird species and is also the only place in Hungary where the lip fern can be found. The Danube-Dráva National Park hosts Hungary's largest osprey nesting site, the highly protected lesser tern, and the unique habitat of two native flowers: the royal fern and the shepherd's cress.

Stalactites in the caves of the Aggtelek National Park entice locals and tourists alike.

INTERNET LINKS

www.eea.europa.eu/soer/countries/hu
This is the European Environment Agency's assessment of Hungary's environment.

www.icpdr.org/main/danube-basin/hungary
The International Commission for the Protection of the Danube River gives an overview of the river in Hungary, including pollution issues.

aqicn.org/map/hungary/
This site provides an interactive, real-time air pollution map of Hungary.

whc.unesco.org/en/list/474/
UNESCO's World Heritage listing of Hortobágy National Park—the Puszta explains the importance of this environmental treasure.

HUNGARIANS

A young Hungarian boy shows off his national pride with the colors of his country's flag painted on his face.

6

ALL PEOPLE ARE DIFFERENT, AND generalizations about any nationality or ethnic group are just that—generalizations. The danger, of course, is in letting such broad descriptions become stereotypes. Nevertheless, many nationalities seem to develop a certain character. Hungarians, in general, see themselves as a small group of unique people who have struggled for many centuries to survive in the midst of other, often hostile, nations. They have a strong sense of national and ethnic pride but are often insecure about their future and place in the world. Although the modern nation is a member of many international organizations, there is still the pervasive sense embedded in the Hungarian identity that Hungary is an island—they are ultimately different and alone.

"When my father was born, it was part of the Austro-Hungarian Empire. When I was born, it was Lithuania. When I left, it was Hungary. It is difficult to say where I come from." —Elie Wiesel (b. 1928) Jewish-American activist and novelist, who was born in Sighet, Maramures—which today is in Romania.

The Carpathian Basin has long been a melting pot for many ethnic groups, and relations between Hungarians and the minorities living in the country have ranged from uneasy to hostile. Among Hungarians there is traditionally a strong division between city dwellers and country people. Sometimes they have less in common with each other than with people of other ethnic groups living in the same town or in a neighboring village.

THE MAGYAR DISTINCTIVENESS

The Magyars took their name from the original seven tribes that settled in Hungary, the Megyers. Hungarians call themselves and their language "Magyar." The term Magyar is also used in English by social scientists to describe ethnic Hungarians. The word Hungarian comes from "Onogur," a Bulgarian-Turkish word meaning ten arrows, referring to the alliance of ten tribes—later seven—that decided to unite and move west to Hungary.

Hungarians pride themselves on their pure and distinctive ethnic heritage. They are usually said to have "Asiatic" facial and physical characteristics, although there has been so much mixing of peoples since the arrival of the Magyar tribes that they are now not much different, in a racial sense, from

Medieval festivals are one of the ways that Hungarians celebrate their shared past.

the peoples around them. What is clear is that the main source of Hungarians' distinctiveness is the preservation of their language over the centuries.

Hungarian is part of the Finno-Ugric family of languages, completely unrelated to any of the Slavic, Romance, or Germanic languages spoken in the surrounding countries. Some Hungarians reject that classification of their language and believe they are at least partly descended from the Sumerians, the earliest civilization in ancient Mesopotamia. They base this idea on some linguistic similarities between their language and some ancient Sumerian writings discovered in the nineteenth century. Most modern linguists dismiss this connection, but either way, Hungarians see the preservation of their language and culture as a critical mission. St. Stephen's acceptance of Christianity and the later struggles against invading Mongols and Turks gave the Hungarians another mission, that of preserving Christianity and Western culture from, ironically, the "barbarians from the East," which the Magyars themselves had once been.

The debate among Hungarians over whether they are essentially "Eastern," and different from Europeans, or "Western," and fully a part of European culture and civilization, has become a major point of division in politics and culture. There is still no agreement over what it means to be Hungarian: nationalists accuse others of being "not Hungarian enough," and are in turn accused of being "not fully European."

THE HUNGARIAN CHARACTER

The question of what is Hungarian was especially sensitive during the years of Communism, when party activists tried to turn Hungarians into "Soviet people." Expressions of national or cultural pride were condemned as "nationalist deviation." During the Kádár era, it became more acceptable to explore the national character. However different groups defined a "good Hungarian" in different or even opposing ways that often excluded other ethnic groups or political opponents from participating in the affairs of the nation.

Pride in being Hungarian leads to a great sensitivity about losing face. Hungarians have never forgotten past instances of national humiliation—

the 1526 defeat by the Ottomans, the failure of the 1848 Revolution, or the forced redrawing of the country's borders in 1920. They are also very sensitive to everyday situations in which they might feel personally humiliated. The word *balek* (BAH-lehk) refers to someone who is cheated, and a balek often appears as the fool in Hungarian cartoons and television shows. Sometimes it seems that Hungarians are constantly watching out for people who might take advantage of them, making them the balek. They have a sense of themselves as victims and feel that others, especially those from the West, can never understand them. Hungarians feel they have contributed to and sacrificed much for the West, yet they are not appreciated as full members of the European or Western community. At the same time, they also are insecure about whether their society, run-down and inefficient after years of Communism, actually deserve to rank with the rest of Europe. They are likely to contrast things, such as the poor service in a restaurant, unreasonable bureaucratic procedures, or a messy room with "the way they do things in Europe."

In spite of those complexities, Hungarians can be very generous to foreigners. They possess an old-world elegance and politeness and will go out of their way to help a stranger. Many are hard-working and full of ambition and creative energy. They can be exuberant celebrants and can also be deeply moved by compassion or the tragedy of fate.

MINORITIES IN HUNGARY

The 2011 census reported that ethnic Hungarians made up 83.7 percent of the population of 9,896,333 people. However, 14.7 percent of respondents did not declare their ethnicity, so the real figure is probably higher. Minorities make up a very small part of the Hungarian population. The Roma are the largest minority at 3.1 percent. Others include Germans, Slovaks, Romanians, and Croats, all at tiny percentages.

JEWS Of the 825,000 Jews who lived in Hungary before the start of World War II, about 565,000 perished during the war, and 260,000 survived. After the war, many Hungarian Jews moved to Israel until the new Communist

Hungarians have always felt an emotional connection with those people who live in the former Hungarian territories that were cut off from the country by the Trianon Treaty in 1920. This feeling was especially strong in the 1970s and 1980s, when there were reports of discrimination against Transylvanian Hungarians in neighboring Romania. The subject of Transylvania is particularly painful, because the northern part of that region was returned to Hungary in 1940 by the Axis Powers during World War II. In 1947, the Allies, having won the war, reversed that decision, and Hungary lost Transylvania once again.

Some Hungarians in Transylvania and elsewhere still live in ethnically uniform villages, cut off from much of the developments of the modern world. They speak old forms of Hungarian and live simple, self-sufficient lives. These people are idealized by nationally-minded Hungarians as the "most Hungarian," in whom Hungarian culture can still be found in its "pure" form, unaffected by the consumer culture of the West. With Hungary becoming more integrated into Western Europe and the international consumer market, many

Ethnic Hungarians living in Transylvania, in Romania, celebrate the Hungarian Revolution with a yearly parade.

Hungarians are traveling to ethnic Hungarian villages in Transylvania to find their cultural roots. It is ironic that they feel they must go beyond Hungary's borders to find the real Hungary.

In 2014, local Roma and their sympathizers march in Budapest with a banner reading "Roma Pride Day" to demonstrate against the racism and discrimination that the Roma community faces in Europe.

government placed restrictions on mass emigrations. During the Hungarian Revolution in 1956, another 20,000 Jews left the country. By the 1970s, the Jewish population had declined to about 60,000, of whom 50,000 lived in Budapest, and more than 60 percent of these people were over the age of fifty.

Today there are between 35,000—120,000 Jewish Hungarians. Though the exact figure is unknown, it is thought to be around 48,000. Most live in Budapest, making it the sixth largest Jewish community in Europe. The Hungarian Constitution guarantees freedom of religion, but anti-Semitism is still a problem. The recent rise of the far-right, nationalist Jobbik Party is concerning, as its members are well known for harboring anti-Semitic views.

ROMA The Roma, or Romani, people—often called gypsies—migrated to Europe from India during the Middle Ages. Census results say that 3.1 percent of Hungarians are Roma, but again, the true numbers are in dispute and may actually be 5—10 percent or higher. Either way, the Roma are the largest of Hungary's minority ethnic groups, and their numbers are growing. The Roma originally made their living as musicians, peddlers, tinkers, and in other door-to-door trades.

Like the Jews, thousands of Roma were rounded up in WWII and exterminated. During the Communist era, the nomadic Roma were forced to settle down, respect borders, and be registered with the authorities. In exchange, they were provided with stable housing and jobs in factories or on agricultural cooperatives. Prejudice against these darker-skinned people remained, however, and they were kept in the lowest-paying, dirtiest, and toughest jobs.

Today, while some Romani Hungarians are active members of society, others remain on the fringes. Many live in illegal shantytowns on the edge of towns and villages, in one-room shacks that lack electricity, water, or sewage connections. Compared to other Hungarians, the Roma are more likely to live in poverty, be uneducated and/or unemployed, and suffer from poor health. They are also widely discriminated against, but the Roma's own clannish culture also contributes in some ways to its marginalization and prevents integration with the rest of Hungarian society.

INTERNET LINKS

www.jewishvirtuallibrary.org/jsource/vjw/Hungary.html
"The Jewish Virtual World: Hungary" is an up-to-date overview of the history of the Jews in Hungary.

www.npr.org/blogs/codeswitch/2014/03/09/287342069/increased-hostility-against-jews-and-roma-in-hungary
NPR, Code Switch: "Increased Hostility Against Jews and Roma In Hungary" explores the rise of nationalism and anti-Roma and anti-Semitic attitudes in Hungary.

www.biography.com/people/groups/hungarian
Bio.com, "Famous Hungarians" offers biographies of some well known Hungarians.

LIFESTYLE

A young couple dances as they enjoy a concert at the Sziget Festival.

7

T HE WAY OF LIFE IN HUNGARY is much the same as it is in most industrialized countries. People go to work, children go to school, and families live together. They enjoy music, sports, gardening, or other hobbies. They have a government that they elected. They live in cities, towns, and the countryside and come from various socioeconomic backgrounds.

Hungarians are literate, and they are well connected: they have mobile phones, smart phones, satellite and cable television, and computers. In general, it seems, most Hungarians would probably say that life in their country for most people is not too bad—perhaps even good—but things could be much better.

CITY LIFE

Many Hungarians in urban areas live in high-rise apartment complexes called *lakótelep* (LAH-koh-teh-lep). These consist of dozens of concrete buildings ten or more stories high and filled with cramped, identical apartments. These developments stand on the edge of towns, and often

The old buildings of Szeged shine in the sun, giving the city its name, which translates to "city of sunshine."

necessitating a long commute to work in the town center. However, the complexes include markets, shops, bars, and other amenities so that, except for work, it is not really necessary to leave them.

Apartments in the lakótelep consist of a tiny bedroom for the children that also serves as a study, and a slightly larger bedroom for the parents that is also the living/dining room. The kitchen holds a stove and a fold-out table at which two can sit, and the bathroom is also tiny. Laundry is hung on the balcony or over the tub, and food, towels, kitchenware, and other necessities are stored in closets along the narrow hall.

Newer and more attractive apartments exist, but they are expensive. Fancier areas of town hold luxurious homes and villas previously occupied by Party officials. Workers' hostels, usually decrepit dormitories for employees at large factories, have largely been sold to private developers or torn down. That, coupled with rising utility prices, has left thousands of people homeless. There are an estimated thirty thousand homeless people in Hungary-about ten thousand in Budapest alone.

In 2012, however, Hungary passed tough anti-vagrancy laws intended to get the homeless off the streets. Begging, sleeping in public areas, and rummaging through trash were outlawed. Unfortunately the government's efforts at cleaning up the city have not extended to providing increased housing for the homeless. Budapest shelters have about 5,500 beds, only half of what is needed.

COUNTRY LIFE

The rural lifestyle is quite different from that of a lakótelep dweller. Hungarian people in the countryside have come a long way since the 1930s; most now live in single-family homes, with a garden attached and a one-acre private plot of land some distance away.

A Hungarian farm on the puszta uses an old fashioned shadoof for collecting water.

Rural people working after hours in their own gardens and private plots have for years produced more than half of Hungary's fruits and vegetables, and a substantial proportion of the country's livestock as well. Village dwellers are thus able to supply most of their own needs, and are envied by many city residents for what they see as a freer and more bountiful lifestyle. On the other hand, most villages lack the cultural and social amenities of the cities, and social life may be restricted to men gathering to drink in a dark, smoky, and dirty *kocsma* (KOHCH-mah) or bar.

SOCIAL ATTITUDES

Although most Hungarians hated communism and neither agreed with nor understood its ideology, the cradle-to-grave communist welfare state left a strong mark on Hungarian attitudes, especially those of the older generation, who had become accustomed to free health care, guaranteed jobs, and even vacations organized for them by their employers. Thus certain attitudes, such as the expectation that the state will take care of every need, are deeply rooted. Some say life was better back then.

On the other hand, perhaps as a reaction to communist attempts to regulate their lives, older Hungarians are very protective of their privacy, are suspicious of highly organized group situations, and prefer to spend evenings at home with a few friends rather than go to a concert or nightclub.

Among the generation born in the late 1980s or after, attitudes reflect a more Western perspective. They hang out with their friends at fast food outlets and other entertainment centers, enjoy rock concerts, and surf the Internet. But at the same time, they are trying to discover and create their own identity as modern Hungarians. The country's problems do weigh on the minds of Hungarian youths. They have little faith in the political system and low expectations of what the government has to offer.

Unemployment among young people is a particular problem. The unemployment rate for people age fifteen to twenty-four is 28.1 percent, which is relatively high. (For comparison, the rate among that age group in Germany is 8.1 percent; and in the United Sates it is 16.2 percent.)

Some young people find themselves attracted to the far-right political parties. Others are just looking for a way out of Hungary. The number of young people leaving the country has doubled since 2010. More young Hungarians want to study abroad, and many want to move away and work elsewhere.

PRIDE AND PREJUDICE

Hungarians are extremely proud of their country and that they managed to preserve their traditions through centuries of war, revolution, and foreign domination. This national identity, while inspiring Hungarians to work together to create their new government and economy, has also given rise to a kind of dangerous nationalism that excludes and even victimizes those who are seen as "outsiders" or "enemies." Increasing competition for scarce jobs has also heightened suspicion of foreigners and minority ethnic peoples.

Jews have traditionally been the target of prejudice in Hungary, due to the belief that they once controlled most of the businesses and commerce. Anti-Semitism has reappeared, in graffiti, in desecrations of Jewish gravestones, and in the writings of populist author and ultranationalist politician István Csurka (1934—2012), who believed that Jews were conspiring with the Americans, the Russians, and the International Monetary Fund to keep Hungary down. That said, Jews in Hungarian society are well established, very integrated, and able to defend themselves through political or legal means.

Another target of much prejudice is the Roma, who are at the bottom of

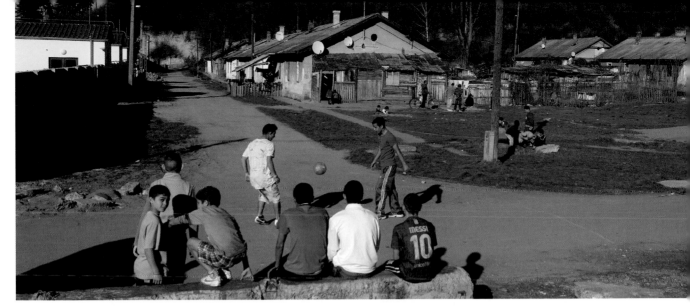

the social ladder and still lead a mostly separate life from the Magyar majority. They are disadvantaged in the areas of health care, housing, employment, and education, and are blamed for rising crime, violence, and other social problems. Skinhead youths have taken to attacking Roma, along with African and Asian immigrants. Some people from surrounding countries have also been victimized. Nationwide campaigns are now underway to improve relations between Roma and other Hungarian peoples.

Some Roma boys kick a ball around in a poor community in Ozd.

CHILDREN AND FAMILIES

Hungarian families have been getting smaller, shrinking from two children down to one child per family, especially in the urban areas. Nevertheless, Hungarians maintain deep bonds with their families. They spend holidays together, send greetings for birthdays and name days, and keep in touch with all their relatives on a regular basis. Children rarely break off contact with parents. Even if family members are no longer on speaking terms, they usually keep informed about each other. Family members are expected to help each other get around the obstacles of daily life and to drop everything to provide necessary assistance in a crisis.

The divorce rate in Hungary is quite high. The divorce:marriage ratio in 2010 was 67 percent, one of the highest in the world. Statistically, this means that in one year, for each population of one thousand people, there were 3.6 marriages, and 2.4 divorces.

EDUCATION

Every Hungarian has the right to an education. Since the 1990s, Hungary's education system has been reformed. The communist-oriented view of history, politics, and philosophy and the compulsory study of Russian were replaced with a broadened, Western-oriented perspective. Private and church-run schools have also reopened.

Students work at their desks in a typical classroom in Budapest.

Free compulsory public education lasts for twelve years and, for most children, begins at age three. Students progress from primary (elementary) school to secondary (high) school. After the eighth grade, some students continue at the *gimnázium* (GIM-nah-zee-uhm), or academic high school, and others go to a vocational high school, where they are trained for mid-level positions in industry, agriculture, trade, or health care. Some students attend skilled worker training schools. Closely tied to specific industries, these include on-the-job training. The rest join the work force. More than half the graduates of secondary schools attend university or college. Many people go to night school or take correspondence courses while working.

Hungary's education system has produced fourteen Nobel Prize winners since 1905. The first Nobel laureate was Philipp E.A. von Lenard for physics in 1905, while the co-recipient of the 2004 Chemistry prize, Avram Hershko, spent his formative years in Hungary before migrating to Israel. Even during the Communist years, important advancements were made by Hungarians in the international fields of medicine, physics, and chemistry.

WOMEN'S ROLES

Legally, Hungarian women enjoy equal protection under the law, and the government supports the principle of equality between the sexes. Traditionally, though, the Hungarian social system is very patriarchal, particularly in rural areas where people are more likely to stick to old ways.

SMOKING IN HUNGARY

In Hungary, as in many other Western countries, the government is trying to reduce smoking. In 2010, more than twenty thousand people died as a direct result of smoking in Hungary. In 2012, a new law went into effect banning smoking in enclosed public places. That year, about 28 percent of the population smoked daily—32.3 percent of men and 23.5 percent of women. In order to make it harder for young people to obtain cigarettes, a new law restricted sales of tobacco products to only designated National Tobacco Stores. There had been more than forty thousand of privately-owned tobacco shops in the country prior to the law, but afterward, the number was reduced to fewer than six thousand. In addition, the price of tobacco products was raised significantly.

Statistically, the law seems to be helping. In one year, the rate of adult smoking dropped to 19 percent. (For comparison, the 2013 rate in the United States was about 17.8 percent.) How much of an impact the law makes on underage smoking is yet to be determined.

According to these views, the man is the head of the household-the provider who makes the important decisions for the family. Women are expected to handle childcare and household chores. Today, men often feel self-conscious about carrying out the tasks traditionally performed by women. Hungarian women still perform 80 percent of household tasks, even if they have a job outside the home.

The country's new constitution, adopted in 2011, asserts that life begins at conception. This might lead to stricter abortion laws in the future. As of 2015, the law allows abortions up to the twelfth week pregnancy.

After a child is born, mothers enjoy a government subsidy that encourages them to stay home with the baby for three years. However, this allowance is small and assumes the father is bringing in a sufficient amount of income. For women without that support, the situation can be very difficult. In Hungary, part-time jobs are hard to find, and mothers may be forced to choose between a full-time job and no job at all. Therefore the employment rate of women with small children is 35—45 percent lower than the EU average.

Hungarians love their palinka, and other alcoholic drinks as well. Naturally, that doesn't mean all Hungarians drink too much. In fact, almost half don't drink at all, and certainly not everyone who does drink is an alcoholic. However, Hungarians consume more alcohol than the average European—and twice the global average.* The trend is similar among other Eastern European countries, including Ukraine, Belarus, and Russia. (Different studies cite different amounts of alcohol consumed per person per year, but Hungary is always in the upper ranks.)

Some say drinking alcohol is engrained in Hungary's working culture. In eastern Hungary, a rural region that has had the country's highest unemployment rate, some people—especially older folks—have a shot of palinka, a popular, very strong fruit brandy, for breakfast. Some old timers consider it to be a tonic, an invigorating boost to their health. Many farmers make a living growing and distilling plums and peaches for the drink.

Certainly drinking has its place in the European lifestyle, but alcohol causes health problems, not the least of which is alcoholism itself. According to the World Health Organization (WHO), in 2012, Hungary had one of the highest rates of alcoholism in the world: 19.3 percent of the population abused alcohol in some form, and as many as 32.2 percent of Hungarian men and 6.8 percent of women suffered from alcohol-use disorders. Hungarians also suffered the highest death rate from cirrhosis, a liver disease caused by alcoholism.

* In some cultures, drinking alcohol is forbidden, and those nations influence these results.

HEALTH CONCERNS

After the demise of Communism, Hungarians were left with a crisis-ridden society. As a whole, they were in very poor health, though that situation has improved. Still, there are high rates of heart and circulatory diseases, cancer, and cirrhosis of the liver. Between 1960 and 2000, the suicide rate in Hungary was the highest in the world, peaking in the mid-1980s. Although it has decreased since then, most likely due to improved medical treatment, Hungary's suicide rate in 2014 was still among the top ten internationally.

The good news is that in the last half century or so, infant mortality has dropped tremendously. Infant mortality measures the rate at which children die before the age of five. In 1949, it was 91.0, meaning out of a thousand live births in Hungary, ninety-one children died before age five. By 1980, that rate was down to 23.2, and in 2013, it was 5.1. Meanwhile, a person's life expectancy at birth has been rising steadily. Life expectancy is the average number of years a person can expect to live. In 1949, it was 59.3 for men and 63.4 for women. In 2013, those figures had risen to 72 years for men and 78.7 for women. Still these life expectancy numbers are among the lowest in the EU. Worse yet, Roma people have a life expectancy of up to ten years lower than ethnic Hungarians.

INTERNET LINKS

www.euromonitor.com/tobacco-in-hungary/report
Euromonitor International offers an informative summary of "Tobacco in Hungary."

247wallst.com/special-report/2014/05/15/the-heaviest-drinking-countries-in-the-world
This article is an overview of the findings in the WHO's "Global Report on Alcohol and Health 2014."

content.time.com/time/world/article/0,8599,2108389,00.html
This *Time* magazine article, "Why Hungary's Youth Are Angry — and Drifting to the Far Right," also includes links to other interesting news stories about Hungary.

www.businessinsider.com/map-divorce-rates-around-the-world-2014-5
Business Insider has a map of divorce rates around the world.

RELIGION

The Holy Crown of St. Stephen is a national icon.

HUNGARY'S CHRISTIAN ROOTS reach back a thousand years to the founding of the first Hungarian state and the crowning of King Stephen by the Pope. Since then, religion has been crucial in defining the Hungarian identity, and religious struggles have often been tied to the struggles of Hungarians to survive.

During the Communist era, state leaders promoted atheism as the official "religion," and churches, especially the predominant Roman Catholic Church, either cooperated with authorities or suffered with the rest of society. As Communism faded in the 1980s, religion made a comeback as a symbol of anti-Communism and national identity, and church attendance increased.

Hungarians today are curious about religion, but it is not an important part of the life of most younger, urban Hungarians. Among older people and in rural areas, religion still plays a strong role.

RELIGION IN HISTORY

The Magyars brought their own well-developed pagan religious ideas with them into the Carpathian Basin. King Stephen I realized that the adoption of Christianity was essential to the Magyars' long-term survival in Europe, however. When he chose Western (Roman Catholic) Christianity over the Eastern variety (the Eastern Orthodox or

8

During World War II, the Holy Crown of St. Stephen was secretly taken out of Hungary to protect it from the Germans and the Soviets. The crown ended up at Fort Knox in the United States, where it remained until 1979, when President Jimmy Carter controversially returned it to the still-Communist government of Hungary.

Saint Stephen's Basilica, the largest cathedral in Budapest, is an important landmark.

Byzantine Church), his decision put Hungary firmly in the West. Within a few years, Stephen succeeded in converting the whole country to Christianity, by force when necessary. Hungary's later participation in the European religious Crusades against the Ottomans sealed its Christian identity and commitment.

During the sixteenth century, the European Protestant movements against the Catholic Church—called the Reformation—quickly spread to Hungary. The Transylvanian princes who safeguarded some measure of Hungarian autonomy during the more than 150 years of partition between the Ottomans and Habsburgs were mostly Protestants, and Protestantism became identified with the struggle for Hungarian independence against the super-loyal Catholic Habsburgs. Calvinism also became very strong in Hungary, and the eastern Hungarian town of Debrecen became known as the "Calvinist Rome," a center for that denomination of strict, ascetic Protestantism. When the Habsburgs got rid of the Ottomans and became sole rulers of Hungary, they used the Catholic Counter-Reformation movement—a Europe-wide counter-offensive against Protestants—to punish Hungarian desires for independence.

More than two centuries of Habsburg rule succeeded in turning Hungary into a predominantly Catholic country. The attachment to the symbolic crown of St. Stephen proved stronger than opposition to the Habsburgs. The Catholic Church grew into a large landholder and one of the main pillars of economic and political power from the quasi-feudal system of the late-nineteenth century until World War II.

PROTESTANTS AND JEWS

Lutherans in Hungary, despite being in the minority, have contributed much to the country's scholarship, literature, art, science, education, social welfare, and medicine.

Calvinist priest Gönc Gáspár Károli published the first complete Hungarian-language Bible in 1590, which had a lasting influence on Hungarian intellectual life and literature. Although it survived without pastors, teachers, or official churches in many parts of the country for much of its early existence, the Reformed (or Calvinist) Hungarian Church was legalized only in the nineteenth century. It was formally established, at last, in 1881.

The first Jews came to Hungary as early as the third century CE, but most Jews arrived in the late eleventh century. Hungary's Jews were divided into two groups: a very religious Orthodox population lived separately in its own communities, following strict Jewish laws and practices, while a less religious group lived in cities and towns, and took up important positions in the economy and later in society. It was this latter group that most enthusiastically responded to the nineteenth-century proposition to "Magyarize" thus finding acceptance among the nobility. They bought estates and became involved in the government. However, the Holocaust ultimately wiped out most of the Jewish communities in Hungary outside Budapest.

The First Calvinist Reformed Church in Buda.

Most Catholic religious orders were dissolved in 1948, when religious schools were also taken over by the state. About four thousand Catholic associations and clubs were forced to disband. Many clergy were imprisoned and prosecuted for political resistance to the Communist regime. In 1950 about one-quarter of the Hungary's monks and nuns, some 2,500 people, were deported. Authorities banned nearly all of the country's functioning religious newspapers and journals.

Cardinal Joseph Mindszenty (1892–1975), the highest Catholic official in Hungary, was a courageous voice against both Fascism and Communism. He loudly opposed the Communist state takeover of parochial schools, and as a result he was arrested in 1949 and charged with treason, conspiracy and other crimes against the new People's Republic of Hungary. While he was imprisoned, he was tortured into confessing to various criminal activities, including "planning a Third World War." During the 1956 Revolution in Hungary, Mindszenty was freed and given refuge in the American Embassy in Budapest. He lived there for the next fifteen years, unable to leave the grounds for fear of being arrested. In 1971, the Hungarian government worked out a deal with the Vatican, and he was released. He lived in Austria until his death, a lone symbol of opposition to Communism.

Meanwhile, the Communists developed their own rites and ceremonies to replace those traditionally offered by the Church. After the Stalinist era ended, the churches reached an accommodation with the Communist rulers. They were allowed to operate without harassment and even received a certain amount of state support, in exchange for accepting the supreme authority of the Party and the permanency of the Communist system. By this time, Hungarians, not the most religious people in the first place, had largely lost interest in religion, however, and church attendance did not rise beyond a small portion of the population.

COMMUNIST ATHEISM

Communist ideology saw religion as a false promise of heavenly justice that could lead people away from the struggle for real justice on earth. In addition, the church in Hungary had been a firm supporter of the old pre-Communist order. Therefore the existence of a strong church and widespread religious beliefs could not be allowed under the Communist system. The Communists nationalized church institutions and property, and many religious organizations were banned.

RELIGIOUS REVIVAL AND NATIONAL IDENTITY

As the Communist system fell apart in the 1980s, people turned to the church for new ideas. Because of the willingness of the past Hungarian church authorities to compromise with the Communists, however, the church in Hungary received much less respect and played a much smaller role in the breakdown of the Communist system than in Poland, Romania, East Germany, and Czechoslovakia.

Stephen I, first King of Hungary, is revered as a saint.

Where religion did play a big role, and continues to do so, is on the symbolic level. The Christian religion has long been tied to the idea of Hungarian national independence through the Holy Crown of St. Stephen. The crosses that many young people wore in the late 1980s thus symbolized not only the rejection of communist atheism, but also loyalty to the Hungarian nation and its independence. The MDF party successfully used religious symbolism to present itself as the truest representative of Hungarian values and win the 1990 elections.

Today the government allows the free practice of religion. In 2002 the government paid religious groups 5.64 billion HUF, or Hungarian forints, (about $20,500 at 2015 conversion rates) as compensation for the assets confiscated during the Communist regime.

The national 2011 census found that 39 percent of Hungarians identified

One of the first things the new freely elected Parliament did in 1990 was to restore Hungary's traditional coat-of-arms. This national symbol—called a címer (TSEE-mehr) in Hungarian—is also known as the Lesser Coat of Arms, and was determined by a Royal Order in 1874 and confirmed in 1895 and 1916.

The címer is topped by the crown of St. Stephen, the symbol of Hungarian nationhood. The bottom right side contains a silver patriarchal cross coming out of a gold coronet. This "apostolic" double-cross became the sign of King Stephen I, representing the religious authority bestowed upon him by Pope Sylvester II and his mission to convert the pagan Hungarians to Christianity.

Born a pagan in the village of Esztergom, Prince Stephen was baptized at the age of ten. King Stephen was zealous for the conversion of his people to Christianity, establishing episcopal sees and monasteries, such as the Benedictine Abbey of Pannonhalma and the center of the Hungarian Catholic Church in Esztergom. Christianity was established as the state religion and pagan practices

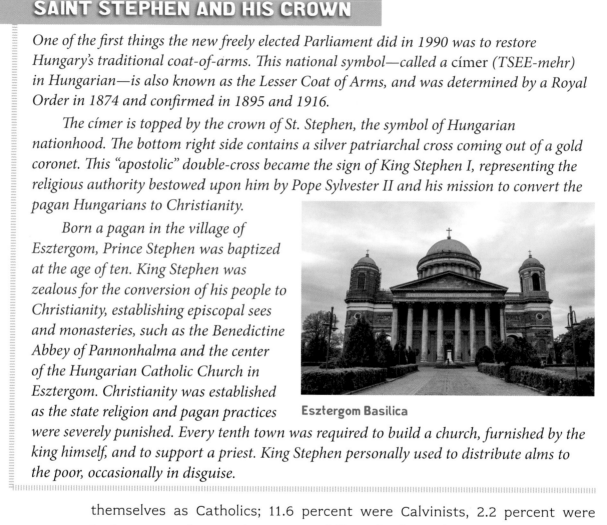

Esztergom Basilica

were severely punished. Every tenth town was required to build a church, furnished by the king himself, and to support a priest. King Stephen personally used to distribute alms to the poor, occasionally in disguise.

themselves as Catholics; 11.6 percent were Calvinists, 2.2 percent were Lutherans, and around 2 percent followed other religions. Of those, Jews made up about 0.1 percent. In addition, 16.7 percent were non-religious, and of those, 1.5 said they were atheists. Another 27.2 percent did not declare a religious identity.

Eastern Orthodox churches have maintained a presence in Hungary since the tenth century. There are now about 13,700 Orthodox Christians in Hungary, including Serbian, Romanian, Hungarian Orthodox, and Bulgarian Orthodox. The western two-thirds of Hungary is largely Roman Catholic, while the Protestants and Eastern Orthodox are mostly found in the east.

Hungary now officially recognizes more than fifty different religions, providing them with state funding in proportion to their size. In addition to those listed above, some religions not traditionally found in Hungary benefit from this policy, including Buddhism and Islam. The latter was recognized by the state in 1916, but was subsequently banned in 1949. Since the late 1980s, Islam has started to return to Hungary.

INTERNET LINKS

hungary.usembassy.gov/holy_crown.html
The US Embassy in Budapest recounts the story of the Crown of St. Stephen and its return to Hungary in 1978.

www.history.com/this-day-in-history/cardinal-mindszenty-of-hungary-sentenced
The History Channel's "This Day in History" entry for Feb. 8, 1949, focuses on the day Cardinal Mindszenty was convicted and sentenced in Hungary.

www.catholicculture.org/culture/library/view.cfm?recnum=10004
This is an overview of Cardinal Mindszenty's life and the situation in Hungary under Communism, from a Catholic point of view.

www.state.gov/j/drl/rls/irf/religiousfreedom/index.htm
This report, "The International Religious Freedom Report for 2013," issued by the US State Department, is a bit dense but is worth picking apart for an up-to-date look at the status of religion in Hungary.

budapestbeacon.com/featured-articles/balog-auschwitz-can-never-happen-again
The Budapest Beacon's "Balog: Auschwitz can never happen again," is an interesting look at Hungarian minister Zoltan Balog's comments on the 70th anniversary of the liberation of the Auschwitz concentration camp.

LANGUAGE

Newspapers on a newsstand in Budapest display the Hungarian language.

9

HUNGARIANS DO NOT CALL themselves "Hungarians," nor do they call their country "Hungary." These are English words. In the Hungarian language, the name of the people is *magyarok* (MUHD-jyor) and their country is *Magyarország* (muh-dyar-ROR-sag, with rolling r's).

The Hungarian language is unique and sounds strange to the untrained ear. Hungarians are proud of the individuality of their language; it forms a major part of their identity. Hungarian is difficult to learn, and few foreigners make the effort, so throughout history Hungarians have always had to use other languages—Latin, German, Russian, and English—to communicate with the outside world.

THE UNIQUE MAGYAR TONGUE

The native Uralic language (the Finno-Ugric branch) brought by the Magyar tribes was later influenced by the Turkic language spoken by the Turkish Ottoman Empire that ruled most of Hungary in the sixteenth and seventeenth centuries. Several hundred words, mostly related to farming, were borrowed from the agricultural Slavic tribes that the Magyars themselves conquered when they occupied the Carpathian Basin. Further influences were later provided by Slovakian, Serbian, and the other surrounding Slavic languages, as well as by Latin, French, and—on the force of the several hundred years of domination by the

"Hungarian Language – savage it may be but of a beauty that has nothing human about it, with sonorities of another universe, powerful and corrosive, appropriate to prayer, to groans and to tears, risen out of hell to perpetuate its accent and its aura ... words of nectar and cyanide."
—Emil Cioran (1911–1995), Romanian writer

The Hungarian alphabet uses the Latin alphabet, along with diacritics (accent marks) on the vowels. The alphabet also includes some "letters" that are groups of letters but are regarded as one: a, á, b, c, cs, d, dz, dzs, e, é, f, g, gy, h, i, í, j, k, l, ly, m, n, ny, o, ó, ö, ő, p, q, r, s, sz, t, ty, u, ú, ü, ű, v, z, zs.

Austrian Habsburg Empire—German. In spite of all these pressures and influences, the basic character of the Hungarian language remained unique and unchanged. Hungarian today is a linguistic island: a language of Asian origin molded by European history.

CONTRIBUTIONS TO ENGLISH Hungarians pride themselves on their language's contributions to English. These include the word coach (in the British sense of bus or carriage) from the Hungarian *kocsi* (KOH-chee), which itself is a derivative of Kocs, the town where a special kind of horse-drawn vehicle was made. Paprika and hussar (from the Hungarian *huszár*, a light calvary soldier) are other contributions.

THE CHARACTER OF THE LANGUAGE

Hungarian is an agglutinative language, meaning that easily recognizable word stems are expanded by adding prefixes and suffixes to create expressive compound words. There are no prepositions; relationships such as in, on, at, and around are expressed by suffixes, as are possession and the identity of the subject or the object of the sentence.

Another idiosyncratic aspect of the language is word order. Hungarians tend to start their sentences with the things they feel need to be emphasized most at that particular moment. This is very flexible. Depending on the context, the sentence "John gave Mary the cat" could just as well be "John the cat gave Mary," or even "Gave John Mary the cat." Hungarians know whether a word is a subject or an object by its suffix, not by its place in the sentence.

The Hungarian language also makes no distinction between male and female. The pronoun *o* stands for both he and she. This does not mean, though, that Hungarian is less "sexist" than other languages. Any woman holding an occupation or position must be identified by adding *no* (woman) to the title (e.g. *tanárno*, from *tanár* and *no*, teacher-woman).

LANGUAGE AND NATIONALITY

In the early nineteenth century, a group of intellectuals made writing and speaking in Hungarian a national campaign. For example, during an 1825 Parliamentary discussion on encouraging the growth of the Hungarian language and culture, young Count István Széchenyi took to the floor and, speaking in Hungarian, offered to found a Hungarian Academy of Sciences to advance the cause. By the late nineteenth century the joint efforts of poets and politicians had established Hungarian as the dominant language.

The Hungarian language became the definer of Hungarian nationality. In order to secure a Hungarian majority in the territory, Hungarian citizenship was offered to anyone who would adopt the language. Thus, to this day, a "true Hungarian" is defined in terms of allegiance to the Magyar tongue as one's first and primary language. Hungarians tend to be very concerned that their language be spoken and written "correctly."

Hungarian has eight dialects, with two spoken outside Hungary's borders, all mutually understandable. Hungarians living in a Transylvanian village may speak an "older" form of Hungarian, but it can still be immediately understood by someone from Budapest.

GREETINGS

Hungarians are very formal and proper in their relations with each other. In pre-Communist times, numerous titles and corresponding forms of address were used to precisely define the ranking of all of society, from the king down to the lowliest serf. During the Communist period, the old forms of address were abolished in favor of the universal *elvtárs* (EHLV-tarsh), or "comrade."

A sign in downtown Budapest helps non-Hungarian-speaking tourists with picture icons.

Hungarians refer to any adult by the formal *ön*, until or unless invited to use the informal *te*. Thus neighbors will often use the formal address with each other for years, and married people generally address their in-laws formally for the rest of their lives. Younger adults are less formal with each other, and tend to use the te form without hesitation. When in doubt, however, Hungarians always choose the formal version to avoid embarrassment or insult. An older form of the formal address, *maga* (MAH-gah), can sometimes be heard when a person wishes to distance themselves from the person being addressed. A boss, for example, might address his employee or servant as maga. This form can also be used as an insult.

MINORITY LANGUAGES

Although there are educational opportunities available in minority languages (German, Slovakian, and Romanian), members of these groups often speak Hungarian better than they do their "native" tongue. Still, street and shop signs are found in these second languages in villages that have a large proportion of minorities.

The Roma form the biggest linguistic minority in Hungary, but only one third of the Roma people speak solely their own language, Romany (a relative of ancient Sanskrit, brought from India, the Roma's original home). In the eighteenth century, the Roma were not allowed to use Romany and had to learn Hungarian instead. Recently the language has seen something of a revival. Since 1998 it has been taught in schools to a majority of Roma students.

FROM RUSSIAN TO ENGLISH

During the Communist period, learning Russian was mandatory for all Hungarian schoolchildren starting in the fifth grade. Students who continued to high school would end up studying Russian for eight years or more, but they were proud to forget most of the language of the Soviet occupiers within a few short years of leaving school.

In 1990, the new government abolished the compulsory study of Russian, and now students may choose from a number of Western languages instead. Today, Hungarians are eager to learn Western European languages, especially English and German. Increased knowledge of these two languages has helped Hungary adapt to Western culture and enter the international business arena.

Private language schools, with names like "London Language Studio" or "Boston Language School," have sprung up all over the capital and can be found in many smaller towns as well. Many young Hungarians can speak English and are eager to practice the language whenever they get the opportunity. Older people are more likely to know German or, of course, Russian.

INTERNET LINKS

www.omniglot.com/writing/hungarian.htm
Omniglot offers an introduction to Hungarian and many links to lessons, phrases, and dictionaries.

www.fluentin3months.com/hungarian-is-easy
An unorthodox, fun look at why, in the author's opinion, Hungarian is easy to learn.

travel.cnn.com/all-hungarian-me-udvozoljuk-one-europes-trickiest-languages-332111
CNN's article, "Üdvözöljük to Hungarian, one of Europe's most curious languages" is humorously informative (and of the opposite opinion to the listing above).

ARTS

Colorful folk art embroidery adorns traditional Hungarian clothing on display in Budapest.

10

THE ARTS IN HUNGARY HAVE A LONG tradition of confronting the country's two constant problems: the lack of national independence and the absence of social justice. For centuries, the arts—especially literature—have played a major role in social movements and, at key points in Hungarian history, have been the spark that set off revolutions.

The Lonely Cedar (1907) is one of the most popular paintings by Hungarian painter Tivadar Kosztka Csontváry.

"I was lucky to have grown up in Hungary, a country that lives and breathes music—that has a passionate belief in the power of music as a celebration of life."
—Sir Georg Solti (1912–1997), world-famous orchestra conductor

LITERATURE AND THE NATION

The best-known examples of early Hungarian literature are the *Gesta Hungarorum*—chronicles by a monk, known only as "Anonymus," which tells the story of the Magyars' migration, settlement, and development up to around 1200 CE—and the works of the first great Hungarian poet, Janus Pannonius, the star of King Matthias Corvinus's fifteenth-century court.

The first major poet to write verse in Hungarian instead of Latin was Bálint Balassi, who started a tradition of lyric poetry in the sixteenth century. He died defending the holy city of Esztergom from the Ottomans. In occupied Hungary during the sixteenth and seventeenth centuries, poets kept the nation's spirit alive by spreading news from fortress to fortress.

The two centuries of Habsburg rule were a setback for Hungarian literature—because educated Hungarians of that era spent most of their time abroad. A new wave of literary rebellion arose, however, following Emperor Joseph I's 1784 proposal to make German the country's official language. Writers such as Ferenc Kazinczy, who rejuvenated the language with modern words, József Katona, whose *Bánk bán* (*Regent Bank*) qualifies as the first great Hungarian drama, and poet Ferenc Kölcsey, whose "*Himnusz*" ("Hymn") became the Hungarian national anthem, all focused on improving and glorifying the Hungarian language in the service of national unity. The Revolutionary Era of 1848 produced Hungary's most beloved poet, Sándor Petofi.

A plaque commemorates the poet Bálint Balassi,

INNOVATION AND POPULISM

The early twentieth century saw a new phase in Hungarian writing with Endre Ady's *New Poems*. He combined modernist ideas with traditional national values. The result was a strange yet beautiful style of writing imbued with political ideas opposing war and the oppression of peasants.

Writers flocked to Paris and other European capitals to sample the new, avant-garde creative movements of impressionism, expressionism, modernism, and, later, dadaism. The literary focus shifted from traditional settings in the countryside to the more urban Budapest. A new, cosmopolitan style befitting a modern European capital developed, as illustrated by the journal *Nyugat* ("*West*"), a potpourri of poetry, short stories, serialized novels, essays, news, political commentary, and translations of foreign literature.

After World War I, a group of young writers and students started exploring the countryside, looking for "the real Hungary." What they found was appalling poverty. Out of these "village explorers" came the populist movement, which has remained a major force in Hungarian literature to this day. Gyula Illyés produced probably the finest example of these writings, *People of the Puszta*.

The cosmopolitan writers of Budapest, on the other hand, were the urbanists, who took the city and the whole world as their subject, and who grouped around the *Nyugat* and other journals. One urbanist who achieved immortality in Hungarian literature was the tragic poet Attila József.

During the years of communism, well-known writers included Gyorgy Konrád and Péter Esterházy, and László Nagy and István Vas were known for their poetry. Post-1989 poets include János Térey, Krisztián Peer, and Dániel Varró, while András Cserna-Szabó is noted for his short stories. In 2002, Imre Kertész became the first Hungarian to be awarded the Nobel Prize for Literature.

Hungarian writer Imre Kertesz poses with his 2002 Nobel Prize for Literature during the awards ceremony in Stockholm.

MUSIC

Hungarian music is a product of two traditions: the mainstream classical European tradition, and a unique, "Asian" type of native music. The Rákóczi

Singer Janos Kobor of the Hungarian band Omega performs at a concert in Berlin, Germany, in 2012.

Rebellion of the eighteenth century generated a characteristic form, the *kuruc* song, which was passed on from one generation to the next.

Franz (*Ferenc*) Liszt, Hungary's most famous pianist and composer, masterfully married European Romanticism with native musical traditions. He consistently used Hungarian themes, both musical and historical, in his compositions. Born in 1811 of a Hungarian father and an Austrian mother, Liszt got his musical education in Vienna and spent much time in Germany and Italy.

Zoltán Kodály and Béla Bartók were the twentieth-century heirs of Liszt's legacy. Kodály, perhaps Hungary's favorite composer, devoted himself to general music education. His persistent advocacy for making music more widely available helped spread an appreciation of music to all Hungarians. Since Kodály, Hungarian music has been characterized by the competent and prolific production of standard classical works, based around such institutions as the Liszt Ferenc Music Academy, the Budapest Philharmonic, the Hungarian Radio Choir, and the Franz Liszt Chamber Orchestra. The isolation of the Stalinist years and the general discouragement of innovation caused the greatest names in Hungarian music since Kodály, such as György Ligeti, to emigrate and make their careers abroad.

Though it was difficult under Communism, Hungarians also produced jazz artists, such as trumpeter Rudolf Tomsits, and rock groups of their own. The bands Illés and Metró were popular in the 1960s and 1970s, and the most successful band, Omega, found international fame and still performs today,

DELIRIOUSLY LISTENING TO LISZT

Long before there was Beatlemania—the intense fan frenzy for the 1960s British rock band—there was Lisztomania. For a few years starting in 1839, when Franz Liszt played piano recitals throughout Europe, a strange phenomenon occurred. Audience members, particularly women, became ecstatic or even hysterical while listening to his music.

It wasn't just the music they were responding to; Liszt was a dynamic performer who played with great physicality. He whipped his head emotionally, vigorously sending his shoulder-length hair flying. It also didn't hurt that the young musician was quite handsome. Women would throw clothing onstage, and after the concert they would literally attack the man, tearing at his clothes and snipping locks of his hair.

Such behavior was far from normal for refined European concert audiences, and German writer Heinrich Heine coined the phrase "Lisztomania." Doctors at the time considered it a mania indeed, an actual physical or mental illness. Today, of course, crazed and exuberant fans are a commonplace sign of celebrity, or rock-star status.

BÉLA BARTÓK: A HUNGARIAN ORIGINAL

Classical and modernist composer Béla Bartók (1881–1945), together with his colleague Zoltán Kodály, spent his summers traveling to small villages and rural settlements to collect samples of genuine folk melodies. They asked village elders to sing the songs they remembered, recording the results on wax cylinders. Their efforts saved Hungary's vanishing folk music traditions. Today, more than 100,000 different recordings are classified and preserved in the archives of the Hungarian Academy of Sciences.

Bartók, like Kodály, saw native melodies as the deepest expression of the "true Hungarian soul." He often incorporated his Hungarian collections—as well as those he made of the melodies of neighboring Slovakians, Romanians, Bulgarians, and Turks—into his music, which ranged from simple folk songs to sophisticated modernist compositions. Unlike Kodály's, Bartók's music never became a favorite of Hungarian listeners; it was often perceived as difficult and strange. But pieces such as his Mikrokosmos *for the piano, his string quartets, and his later* Concerto for Orchestra *are considered masterpieces of precision, innovation, and individuality. Bartók died in exile in New York in 1945, poor and lonely.*

Bartók's role in Hungarian culture did not end with his death. His music was banned in Hungary during the 1950s, and young people played his records as an act of political opposition.

In 1988, the musician's remains were returned to Budapest for reburial. His body traveled by ship from New York to England and then by motorcade across France, Germany, and Austria, with concerts at major towns along the way. The event dominated the Hungarian media for weeks, and the essentially apolitical composer was celebrated all at once as a populist, an antifascist, an advocate for minority rights, a national hero— and, almost as an afterthought, as a musician.

a half century after its founding in the 1960s. Today, Hungarian radio stations carry everything from smooth jazz to world music to funk, electronica, pop—and classical, of course.

COMMUNISM AND CULTURE

The arts in Hungary in the early 1950s were dominated by "socialist realism," meaning that all art had to reflect the reality of the "socialist person." Short stories and novels told of workers or peasants overcoming doubts and learning to work harder for Communism, eventually joining the Party and vowing to work even harder in the future. Paintings and sculptures likewise turned to depictions of strong, self-sacrificing, heroic workers holding the Communist flag high. Even in poetry and music, odes to Soviet leader Joseph Stalin, or to Hungarian leader Mátyás Rákosi, were preferred. Some writers were able to preserve their integrity by writing "for the desk drawer"—works that could not possibly be published at the time, but that might be able to appear in the future if the system ever changed.

The Kádár era (1958–1988) was one of compromise and liberalization. Much more was allowed to be published, produced, and shown than previously, although there were certain very firm limits. No criticism of the Soviet Union or the Soviet-Hungarian alliance was allowed, nor of the socialist system or of the leading role of the Communist Party in political life. Private matters, such as love, death, and family life, were free territory, and social problems could even be brought up if done carefully. Writers learned the limits of what was allowed, restraining themselves just enough to avoid the risk of crossing the line and being persecuted.

PAINTING

Hungarian painting has been much less important than literature in the development of the nation, and has gained much less international recognition than Hungary's musicians and composers. Hungary's history of foreign occupation made it difficult for artists to find the support they needed to develop a characteristic national style. When a demand arose

"I carry a deep sadness of the heart which must now and then break out in sound." —Hungarian composer and pianist Franz Liszt (1811–1886), toward the end of his life when he was in poor health.

A HUNGARIAN EXPRESSIONIST

In 1881 a young pharmacist in the southern Hungarian town of Pécs experienced a vision. God appeared before him and told him to go to the ends of the earth and paint the spiritual wonders he saw. Tivadar Csontváry Kosztka set off to fulfill this destiny. The paintings he produced in the next few years show mystical and religious subjects, strange and symbolic figures, and seductive colors, often painted on huge canvasses. Kosztka

painted wondrous scenes from Sicily, Lebanon, Jerusalem, Switzerland, and the Hungarian puszta.

His paintings all exhibit the painful gap between his mad, holy visions and the desolate reality of human life as he saw it. Although his work has been classified as expressionist, it shows signs of primitivism and naturalism, and even of the future trends of art nouveau and surrealism.

Kosztka's genius was little recognized during his wandering lifetime. He was "discovered" in the 1920s, after his death, and again in the 1950s. In recent years, his paintings have become extremely popular among younger Hungarians. Prints of Kosztka's paintings, such as The Lonely Cedar *(1907) or* Pilgrimage to the Cedars of Lebanon *(1907) can often be seen gracing the walls of Hungarian lakótelep apartments, perhaps representing the romantic hopes and often difficult realities of such apartment dwellers.*

for paintings in the nineteenth century, Hungarian artists did little more than imitate the styles current in Vienna or France, especially classicism. At most, they took Hungarian historical events or personalities for their subjects.

Mihály Munkácsy was probably the most renowned of these nineteenth-century painters, although he spent much of his creative life in Paris. The prolific post-impressionist painter József Rippl-Rónai helped keep Hungarian art up-to-date at the turn of the twentieth century.

THE FILM INDUSTRY

After 1958, the Hungarian film industry was reorganized and, surprisingly, given a large amount of freedom to explore new and critical themes. Miklós Jancsó, one of Hungary's greatest directors, made *The Round Up* in 1965. It was about Hungarian peasants being forced to act as collaborators and traitors during the 1848 Revolution, a theme that paralleled the humiliation of the peasantry in the 1950s. The Stalinist years became a frequent topic, whether of critical dramas, cutting farces, or hard-hitting documentaries.

In the 1980s the financial plight of the state studios forced them to enter into coproduction agreements with West European studios. István Szabó, Hungary's most prominent director, used this situation to make films that were implicitly critical of his country's political system, and which would be seen by international audiences. An example is the 1981 Oscar-winning *Mephisto*, about a German artist who sells his soul to the Nazis—an easily understood parable about the compromises made by his fellow Hungarian artists under the regime of János Kádár.

A distinction of the Hungarian film industry is the prominent role of women directors, of whom Márta Mészáros is the best-known, in making documentaries and dramas that deal especially with the problems of women in Hungarian society. After 1989, a new wave of directors emerged, such as

Hungarian film director Miklós Jancsó is shown in 2012 at age ninety.

The facade of a New York City street scene is a movie set at Korda Studios in Hungary.

Kornél Munruczó, György Pálfi, and Benedek Fliegarf.

Hungary has also become a popular place for international filmmakers to make movies, thanks in part to strong tax incentives. Budapest, which has been nicknamed "Hollywood on the Danube," can reportedly be made to look like any number of European cities, making it a prime filming location. The city is home to several world-class movie studios. For example, Korda Studios opened in 2007, boasts one of the world's biggest soundstages and impressive backlot sets, including a New York City set built for the 2008 movie *Hellboy II: The Golden Army*.

TRADITIONAL ARTS AND CRAFTS

The most characteristic Hungarian craft forms are embroidery, pottery, and carving. Elaborate embroidery, featuring flowers, leaves, birds, and spiral designs, was traditionally required for a peasant bride's dowry, which might include a dozen ornate pillows and embroidered sheets, two to four decorated feather quilts, and six to eight elaborate tablecloths.

After the fall of Communism, many Hungarians wanted to remove all traces of the hated system from everyday life. The statues put up by the Communists were an obvious target, and plans were made to put all of the capital's Communist monuments in a Szoborpark ("Statue Park."). The task of cutting down and removing these massive figures of granite and bronze proved to be more difficult, and far more costly, than anyone thought. Many people complained that, in a time of increasing hardship, the money should be used for more pressing social needs.

There were also philosophical and political disputes. Some argued that the symbols of forty years of oppression should be "wiped off the face of the earth." Others felt that they had become a basic and inseparable part of the city's landscape and should be left to stand, along with monuments from previous eras. Russia protested at the "desecration" of memorials to Red Army soldiers who fell on Hungarian soil during World War II. It was charged that the removal of a statue of the 1919 revolutionary Béla Kun was in effect a tribute to the repressive Horthy regime that drove Kun out. One group of veterans of the 1956 uprising got so carried away that they toppled a statue of the Greek goddess Nike because the five-pointed star she carried resembled the Communist red star.

After three years of debate and preparation, Memento Park opened in the spring of 1993. It holds forty-two prime examples of socialist realist sculpture from all over Budapest on a 20-acre (8-hectare) expanse. Huge figures of Marx and Lenin, of the traditional socialist worker-hero, of Soviet soldiers, and of obscure Hungarian Communists now have only one another to intimidate. The effect is strange, but the park has become a favorite tourist destination.

Embroidered souvenirs exhibiting the Hungarian folk art style are for sale at a craft market on Castle Hill in Budapest.

Sárköz in Transdanubia, the Matyó region in the Great Plain, and Kalocsa on the southern Danube are especially well known for their needlework. The Székely people in eastern Transylvania use hides and sheepskins to make thick coats and jackets, which are then lavishly decorated.

Leatherwork and intricate horn carving is the domain of the men of the puszta, who produce canes, whip handles, penknives, flutes, and pipes, featuring everyday scenes and patriotic symbols. The old plains style of ceramics produces pottery smoked black in the kiln, unglazed and varnished with pebbles. Standardized, mass-produced clothes and furnishings have now replaced traditional styles in Hungarian peasant homes, but festivals and special occasions still bring out characteristic costumes.

CRISIS IN THE ARTS

The advent of a free market system after 1990 was a shock to creative artists. Not only did they now have to worry about the commercial side of their art, but a massive influx of cultural products from the West—everything from reality television programs to the Harry Potter novels and the latest Brad Pitt flick—flooded the market and made it even more difficult for Hungarian artistic productions to compete.

The positive side of the change is, of course, the possibility for the Hungarian arts to finally express themselves in complete freedom, without self-censorship or fear. Furthermore, many feel that now creative artists can return to universal themes and pure artistic achievement, thus making Hungarian culture meaningful for all the world.

"This park is about dictatorship. And at the same time, because it can be talked about, described, built, this park is about democracy. After all, only democracy is able to give the opportunity to let us think freely about dictatorship."
—Ákos Eleod, the architect who designed Memento Park in Budapest.

INTERNET LINKS

bartokradio.rad.io
MR3 Bartók Rádió is a radio station in Budapest that broadcasts classical music along with some jazz and news.

www.npr.org/2011/10/22/141617637/how-franz-liszt-became-the-worlds-first-rock-star
NPR has both an audio and transcript version of the story "How Franz Liszt Became The World's First Rock Star."

www.mementopark.hu/
The official site of Memento Park in English is quite well done, informative, and even tongue-in-cheek humorous.

LEISURE

Rubik's Cube was invented by a Hungarian architect.

11

TAKE A WALK, GO FOR A RUN, GET together with friends, catch a movie, surf the net—these are the kinds of things most people do when they have some free time, and Hungarians are no different. People in the big cities, especially Budapest, have a wide array of cultural opportunities, from visiting museums to attending concerts to strolling through beautiful city parks. In rural areas, people with spare time on their hands might putter in the garden, work on a hobby, or do some bird-watching in one of Hungary's national parks. Young people, like their peers everywhere, can catch up on homework, but they would probably prefer to play some *focl* ("soccer") or hang out with friends.

In 1974, Hungarian architecture professor Erno Rubik created a three-dimensional puzzle that he used to explain spatial relationships to his students. His "Magic Cube" went on to become "Rubik's Cube," one of the world's most popular—and frustrating—puzzle toys. There's only one correct answer and 43 quintillion wrong ones! About 350 million cubes have been sold.

SPAS AND BATHS

Hungary has more than a thousand thermal springs, some with temperatures higher than 86°F (30°C). Early Celtic and Roman settlements have been found near springs. The ruins of the Roman regional capital, located outside Budapest, are called Aquincum, from the Celtic *Ak-Ink*, meaning lots of water. The splendid Roman baths were fed by a system of canals and had floor and wall heating. The Magyars also recognized the therapeutic potential of the waters, but it was the Turks who fully harnessed the land's thermal powers and left behind the network that exists today.

Thermal treatments include drinking the water as well as bathing in natural caves, pools, lakes, and elaborately constructed spas. Spas in special locations are recommended for specific ailments, whether arthritis, open wounds, or lung problems. There are even radioactive mud cures. Tourists have flocked to Hungary since as far back as the seventeenth century to take the cures, and many Hungarian town names

At a spa in Budapest, it's not unusual to see people playing chess while bathing.

are recognizable as former or current spa locations by the suffix *fürdo* or *füred*, meaning "bath." The thermal lake at Hévíz is the world's second largest natural hot spa, with a surface area of more than 470,000 square feet (43,664 sq. m). This wonder was once threatened by bauxite mining for Hungary's important aluminum industry, which had siphoned off half of the water that nature previously pumped in, nearly destroying both the lake's healing heat and its ecological balance. Fortunately, bauxite mining in the area has ceased.

The majestic baths of Budapest are meeting hubs as well as places to relax and ease the day's aches and pains. They used to play host to lovers' rendezvous, but strict separation of the sexes since Turkish times put a stop to that. At baths where mixed crowds are allowed, bathing suits must be worn. Otherwise, small "aprons" are handed out to cover the essentials. At some baths, chess players concentrate on boards fixed at the level of the water. One may also want to get a massage, just relax in the steam, or sit and admire the splendid architecture of the spa buildings, ranging in style from Turkish to classical to art nouveau.

SOCCER AND OTHER SPORTS

Ferenc Puskás shows his legendary skills on the field.

Hungarians are devoted sports fans, and membership in sports clubs and associations is very high. Fans avidly read several sports newspapers in order to keep up-to-date on contract negotiations, coaching changes, and gossip about their favorite sports stars, in addition to scores and statistics.

Like all good Europeans, Hungarians are mad for *focl* ("football," meaning soccer, not American football). Fans follow both the national league and international matches. Although the level of league play is not as high as in the larger European countries, Hungary's national teams did very well in the past. Older fans can still recite from memory the names of the players on the legendary "Golden Team" of the early 1950s. The successes of the "Golden Team" gave Hungarians hope that, though their political and social aspirations were suppressed at home, at least in sport they could achieve greatness. Ferenc Puskás (1927—2006) was a particular source of national pride. The football superstar from Budapest is widely considered one of the greatest players of all time—if not *the* greatest. During the 1950s, he was captain of the Hungarian national team, the Mighty Magyars, and later

HUNGARY AND THE OLYMPIC GAMES

Hungary's successes in Olympic competition (mainly in the summer sports) are a source of great national pride. Despite its small size, Hungary has won a total medal haul (as of 2012) of 476 Summer Games medals and 6 Winter Games medals, including 167 gold medals.

Fencing is by far Hungary's strongest Olympic sport. Each time the games come around, the country is gripped by the Olympic fever, and headlines across the press celebrate each Hungarian gold medal.

The country's athletes have also found particular success in modern pentathlon, fencing, gymnastics, wrestling, and water sports. Hungary's swimmers have impressed the world, winning two golds in 2012. The water polo team has taken the gold medal an amazing eight times, and the soccer team won it three times. The modern pentathlon, combining horse riding, fencing, shooting, swimming, and running, is said to present a similar challenge to that faced by Magyar warriors in times past.

Hungary was one of the founding nations of the modern Olympic movement in 1894, and the country has participated in every game since the beginning, with the exception of the 1920 Olympics, when the destruction wrought by World War I and political instability prevented it, and the 1984 Los Angeles Games, when Hungary's political leadership forced its athletes to follow the Soviet-led boycott, disappointing the country greatly. Just three weeks after the tragic events of 1956, Hungarian athletes stoically appeared at the 1956 Melbourne Games and the country placed fourth in the overall medal standing. A measure of national pride was salvaged in the semi-final round of the water polo competition, when Hungary defeated the Soviet Union 4-0 in a game called off early to prevent rioting and fought so hard that the water was said to have turned red from the wounds the players inflicted on each other. The Hungarian team went on to win the gold.

emigrated to Spain to play for the powerhouse team Real Madrid. To this day he is a national hero.

Hungarians also closely follow developments in swimming, water polo, gymnastics, canoeing/kayaking, and fencing, as well as team handball, penthathlon, cycling, sport shooting, basketball, and, in the winter, ice hockey, skating, and cross-country skiing.

Hungarians are also proud of the three chess-playing Polgár sisters, two of whom are ranked grandmasters. Judit Polgár (b. 1976) is considered the strongest female player in the world, and has defeated ten (male) world champions; she retired from competitive chess in 2014.

INTERNET LINKS

www.ifhof.com/hof/puskas.asp
The International Football Hall of Fame has a page devoted to Ferenc Puskas.

www.cnn.com/2014/06/27/travel/hungary-spas
CNN's article "Saunas, soaking and chess: Hungary's best spas" includes great pictures.

visitbudapest.travel/activities/budapest-baths
"Budapest Baths" on this travel site details the city's historic thermal spas.

www.cnn.com/2013/11/19/travel/things-to-know-hungary
CNN's "11 things to know before visiting Hungary" is a fun overview of Hungarian leisure and culture.

www.cnn.com/2012/10/10/tech/rubiks-cube-inventor
"The little cube that changed the world" on CNN includes graphics and an interview with Erno Rubik.

"There is not one Hungarian who would be left untouched by the death of Ferenc Puskás. The best-known Hungarian of the twentieth century has left … Ferenc Puskás has left us, but 'Puskás Öcsi' the legend will always stay with us." —Ferenc Gyurcsány, the Prime Minister of Hungary, speaking about the death of the Hungarian soccer superstar in 2006.

FESTIVALS

Fireworks light up the night on Saint Stephen's Day in Budapest.

12

HUNGARY'S TRADITIONAL HOLIDAYS and festivals were based on the religious and agricultural calendars, including saints' days, and planting and harvest days. The Communist system substituted the traditional holidays with "political" holidays marking landmarks in Communist history. Few believed in these new holidays, but all were forced to recognize and "celebrate" them. With the new post-Communist system, these unpopular holidays have been abolished, and the old traditional ones have been returned to their former importance.

August 20, Saint Stephen's Day, is an official state holiday in Hungary, marking the day Stephen I became the first king of Hungary in the year 1000. In Budapest, the celebration is observed with fireworks over the Danube.

BIRTHDAYS AND NAME DAYS

While birthdays are celebrated in Hungary, they are not nearly as important as "name days." (This is true in much of Europe.) The days on the Hungarian calendar are each assigned to a certain Christian name that is commonly known and used. These assigned days are based on religious traditions, historical events, or birthdays of famous people, so that every name has a name day. In fact, the most common Hungarian

The end-of winter carnival festivities of the Mohács area feature strange and wonderful costumes.

names, such as László, Zoltán, or Zsuzsanna, each have two or even three days assigned to them—Maria has eight! In that case, one of these days is chosen for the child of that name, and family and friends are told to celebrate on that day and not the others. On name days for the most common names, flower-sellers do a fabulous business, and it seems that every second person on the street or subway has a bouquet in hand.

On their appointed name days, Hungarians might receive flowers and a greeting from their fellow students or co-workers. Then, in the evening the lucky Ágnes or János goes home to assembled family members, more flowers, a special dinner, and toasts. Small gifts may be given by the immediate family, but coming together to celebrate is more important. Birthdays are celebrated in a similar way, but with a smaller gathering, and are usually not marked at all by friends or colleagues.

VILLAGE HOLIDAYS AND FESTIVALS

Traditional holidays in the Hungarian countryside mix religious ceremonies with old agricultural traditions. Spring harvest festivities are held in March and April, while August and September are the months for fall harvest celebrations. These events are marked by drinking, eating, and dancing in the open air. Major national and local saints' days are also celebrated, and some villages still hold annual fairs where craftspeople show their wares and there are dances and folk music. Wine festivals are also held in late summer and fall, with much drinking and dancing.

Pre-Lenten or Carnival festivities are uncommon in Hungary, but one place where such customs have remained strong is the area around Mohács in the south of the country. The mourning procession or *busójárás* (BOO-shoh-yah-rahsh) typically features strange costumes, wild and scary animal masks, and the performance of skits to music, ending in general revelry and a large bonfire. These festivals are probably connected as much with ancient rituals to drive away winter and with the expulsion of the Turkish occupiers from Hungary as with the beginning of the Christian fasting period.

Unique Hungarian Easter customs go back to pagan fertility and healing rites. Boys and young men call on young women in the village and sprinkle them with water. In return, the women offer Easter eggs, cookies, and an alcoholic drink. This ritual has been transferred to the city, where the water is replaced by lightly sprayed perfume.

Easter eggs are decorated with intricate folk art designs.

The traditional Easter feast includes baked ham and boiled eggs. Egg-decorating in the village is elaborate and reflects the local craft style. Eggs may be dyed and decorated in folk art motifs, glazed, or have tiny horseshoes hung on them.

CHRISTMAS IN HUNGARY

The Christmas season starts in Hungary on December 6, St. Nicholas's Day. Children put newly polished boots in the window, like the stockings hung by the fireplace on Christmas Eve elsewhere. If the child has been good, Mikulás (or Szent Miklós) leaves the boot filled with goodies—traditionally chocolate, tangerines, apples, walnuts, dates, and figs. If the child has been bad, the boot will contain just a piece of coal, a wooden spoon, a stone, or even a potato or an onion.

The rest of December is filled with school programs, in which parents are invited to come and hear songs, poems, and plays about winter and Christmas. The climax comes on December 24, or *Szenteste* ("Holy Night"). This is a night for the immediate family members to sit around a small Christmas tree, eat and drink together, and exchange gifts. A traditional Christmas tree decoration is the *szaloncukor* (SAH-lon-tsooh-kor)—candy made from fondant or another sweetmeat, wrapped first in tissue paper with fringed ends then a layer of shiny and colorful foil. On the following two days

The Sziget Festival in Budapest is one of the largest music and cultural festivals in Europe. The annual event takes place for a week each August on Óbudai-sziget ("Old Buda Island"), a 266-acre (108 hectare) island in the Danube—sziget means "island"—in the northern Óbuda section of Budapest. The festival began in 1993 as a Woodstock-style rock fest and then expanded even further into a cultural extravaganza not unlike the Burning Man event in the United States. The 2014 festival attracted 415,000 visitors over the course of seven days; more than half of them came from outside Hungary, mainly Western Europe. More than a thousand performances take place each year, including top international and American acts. Past performers have included Prince, Cee-lo Green, Florence and the Machine, José González, Snoop Dog, Macklemore & Ryan Lewis, Outkast, and many others.

(December 26 is also a holiday), the family gets together with other relatives to feast and to eat special cakes, most commonly the *beigli* (BAY-glee), a rolled pastry filled with poppy seeds or nuts.

A village tradition of the Christmas season is *regolés* (REH-goh-lesh), from the name of the ancient songs that children and young men used to sing from door to door, wishing their neighbors good luck and a fruitful harvest in the new year. December 26 and 27 are name days for István (Stephen) and János (John), two of the most common Hungarian names, and so these name days are also incorporated into the Christmas cycle.

The holiday season is topped off by New Year's Eve, which Hungarians call *Szilveszter* (SIL-veh-ster). It's celebrated through drinking, music, dancing, and, at the stroke of midnight, eating *virsli* (VEER-shlee) or sausages. Pork and lentil dishes are traditionally eaten on New Year's Day.

INTERNET LINKS

www.festival.si.edu/2013/Hungarian_Heritage/index.aspx
"Hungarian Heritage: Roots to Revival" was a 2014 festival at the Smithsonian Folklife Festival. This accompanying website has information, photo galleries, and videos about traditional Hungarian arts, crafts, music, dance, and other folkways.

szigetfestival.com
Sziget "Island of Freedom" official site has info, photos, and videos in English.

abouthungary.net/festivals-and-events-in-hungary
This is an up-to-date listing of a wide variety of festivals in Hungary.

www.budapest-discovery-guide.com/hungarian-christmas-traditions.html
"Hungarian Christmas Traditions" is a short overview of the holiday.

FOOD

A baker assembles a seven-layer Dobos Torte, a classic Hungarian cake.

13

WHEN MOST PEOPLE THINK OF Hungarian food, they think of goulash—without even quite knowing what it is. So-called "American goulash," a mix of ground beef, macaroni, and tomato sauce, is nothing like authentic Hungarian goulash, which is a thick, spicy beef soup made red with paprika. Hungarian food is hearty, rich, and meaty. The country's food reflects not only its own nomadic, Asiatic Magyar past but also Turkish, Jewish, Serbian, Austro-German, and American influences. Paprika and goulash have become symbols of Hungarian cuisine.

THE PEPPER

The characteristic ingredient in Hungarian cooking is paprika, which finds its way into almost every Hungarian dish. We know paprika as a spice, the ground, dried red pepper that gives a characteristic flavor and reddish color to most Hungarian dishes. Hungarians also use the word for any fresh pepper, from the "white paprika," through yellow and red,

One of Hungary's most internationally esteemed foods is the *dobostorta* or Dobos Torte, named for its creator József Dobos, a Hungarian confectioner, who introduced it in 1885. The five- or seven-layer cake is made with alternating thin layers of sponge cake and chocolate buttercream, glazed on top with caramel.

Paprika, meaning both whole peppers and the spice made from them, is crucial to Hungarian cooking.

to the small dark red peppers that set the mouth on fire. Fresh peppers are either sweet or hot. The taste, along with the shape and color, guide the shopper in making a selection. Several different types, as well as the ubiquitous powdered form, can appear in one dish, such as *lecsó* (LEH-choh), a common stewed mixture of peppers, tomatoes, and onions, often including sausage or bacon and sometimes scrambled with eggs.

Paprika appeared in Hungary around the sixteenth or seventeenth century. At first, it was used only by the lower classes, who could not afford the "genuine" spices imported from the Far East. Over time, it gradually worked its way up the social ladder and, by the middle of the nineteenth century, became an essential part of Hungarian cuisine. Ever since, paprika has been considered a typically and uniquely Hungarian spice. The pepper helped Hungarian scientist Albert von Szent-Györgyi Nagyrapolt win the Nobel Prize in physiology or medicine in 1937 when he discovered vitamin C in one of its richest sources—paprika.

SOUPS AND STEWS

Hungary's culinary claim to fame is goulash (*gulyás*, GOO-yash, in Hungarian). The dish is cooked with mutton, beef, or pork, and there is even one variation called *hamis* (HAH-mish, fake) with no meat at all. Goulash supposedly dates back to the time of the original Magyar tribes, who cooked meat together with onions and then dried the product, carrying it with them on their marauding expeditions to reconstitute later—the world's first "instant" soup. Goulash has since been traditionally cooked in a special copper or cast-iron kettle called a *bogrács* (BOH-grahch), hung from a stick over an open fire. (The dish might still be served in a restaurant in a mini-bogrács over a flame.)

Hungarian stews called *pörkölt* (PUR-kult) and *paprikás* (PAH-pree-kash) consist of meat (pork, beef, chicken, lamb, veal, or—a Hungarian traditional specialty—wild boar), and might have mushrooms or potatoes. The meat and vegetables are stewed in fat with onions and lots of paprika, and served over small dumplings called *galuska* (GAH-loosh-kah). A paprikás is distinguished by the addition of sour cream, which makes it thicker and richer. Side vegetable dishes served with it include spinach, green peas, or cabbage, either stewed or creamed.

A full Hungarian meal almost always begins with a soup of a lighter variety, such as mushroom, cauliflower, or green pea. These soups are made by briefly sauteeing the main vegetable together with a few pieces of carrot and parsley, adding water and later a *roux* (a thickener) made from oil, onion, flour, and paprika, and finally a pasta called *tarhonya* (TAR-hone-yah), made of flour and egg dough. Other options for the soup course are meat broth made from either beef or chicken, and a Hungarian specialty, cold fruit soup, made from cherries or plums and milk or sour cream. Other Hungarian soups, including *halászlé* (HAL-ahss-lee, "fish soup"), bableves (BAHB-leh-

Hungarian goulash cooks in a traditional bogrács over an outdoor fire.

vesh, "bean soup"), and goulash itself, are substantial enough to be a meal in themselves, and are not usually followed by another main course.

Hungarian cuisine can be spectacularly rich, featuring pork in high proportions, *töpörtyu* (TUH-pur-tchew, pork cracklings), *szalonna* (SAH-lohn-nah, Hungarian bacon eaten straight or with bread), and *zsír* (ZHEER, pork lard used for everything from frying onions for stews and soups to baking cakes and pastries or spreading directly on bread). These are only somewhat balanced by the traditional "salads," which for Hungarians mean pickles, pickled cabbage or peppers, or perhaps sliced tomatoes. Vegetables, if they do appear, are either breaded and fried or cooked almost beyond recognition in a *fozelék* (FUH-zeh-layk, vegetable stew). In addition, the more exotic portions of animals—like pigs' knuckles, liver, kidney, tongue, cow stomach lining, bone marrow, calf's brain, chicken gizzards, or items called simply "inside parts"—are prized delicacies.

DRINKING AND TOASTING TRADITIONS

Hungary's national drink is a clear brandy called *pálinka* (PAH-lin-kah), which can be made from apricots, pears, cherries, plums, grape skins, or a mixture of fruits—to be sampled at one's own risk! (It's definitely a drink for adults only!) Hungarian hosts offer the drink to adult guests or visitors at any time of the day or evening, and it is rude to refuse without a good reason. Pálinka is best served cold and is drunk straight from a shotglass (a shot is a single measure, usually an ounce), in one gulp if possible. *Házi* (HAH-zee, or home-made) pálinka, made by a farmer rather than in a distillery, is especially prized. It may sometimes be replaced by vodka, which Hungarians believe to be a cure for an upset stomach. The fashion for all things Western has brought gin, French brandy, and whiskey into many Hungarian shops and homes, but pálinka remains the hard liquor of choice for the true Hungarian.

Two Hungarian wines have achieved international renown. *Egri Bikavér* (AIG-ree BEE-kah-vair), "Bull's Blood of Eger," is a dark and strong wine from that northeastern valley. *Tokaji* (TOH-kah-yee), the sweet white dessert wine made from grapes around Tokaj, farther east along the Tisza River, has been called "the wine of kings and the king of wines" for its prominence at royal tables over the centuries. The quality, cost, and sweetness of the best tokaji, the Aszú variety, is indicated by the number of *puttonyos* (POO-tohn-yohsh) it contains. A puttonyos is a unit that measures the amount of a paste made from the region's withered, super-sweet grapes. Other fine Hungarian wines, both red and white, are made around Lake Balaton, along the southernmost stretch of the Danube, and near the towns of Pécs and Sopron.

Learning the Hungarian toast—*Egészségére* (EH-gayse-shay-gay-reh), meaning "to your health"—is often a foreign visitor's initiation into the mysteries of the Hungarian language. With this toast, glasses are then clinked and drained. When drinking beer, however, this was not the custom for 150 years. Legend has it that the Austrians who executed the freedom-fighting Hungarian generals of the 1848 Revolution clinked beer glasses as the fatal shots rang out. Only recently have Hungarians started clinking beer glasses again.

SHOPPING AND DINING

Hungarians like to buy their foods fresh, doing most of their shopping at the *piac* (PEE-ahts), or market. It might be a vast indoor market hall, an outdoor brick-walled enclosure, or just a designated open space, filled with rows of sellers of vegetables, fruit, eggs, cheese, meat, and fish. The sellers are sometimes the growers of the food themselves, but more often they buy produce from the grower and resell it. Some stalls offer a wide variety of fruits and vegetables, along with a few packaged products; others are filled with mounds of potatoes, peppers, or melons, which they offer for the best price and sell steadily. Elderly women offering a few carrots, onions, or turnips from their gardens fill the spaces in between stalls. The shopper brings a bag, and the seller, after weighing out the requested quantity—usually by putting metal weights on a manual scale—dumps the produce into the shopper's bag, right on top of what is already there.

A view of the Great Market Hall (*Nagycsarnok*) in Budapest

The piac—which is closed on Sunday and Saturday afternoon—is a lively place. Sellers praise their wares, shoppers debate whether they really got the firmest tomatoes or the freshest mushrooms, and there is often a beer stand or two full of thirsty customers. All kinds of non-food items are hawked around the outskirts. Western, mainly Austrian and German, chains are opening more and more supermarkets in Hungarian cities and towns. Offering a wider and more appetizing selection than Hungarian markets, they are especially popular with those who have more money to spend and less time to search the piac for the best bargains. Since fruit and vegetable stands can be found everywhere, even near bus stops and at busy street corners, and most families have little storage space in their refrigerators, shopping often for fresh food remains the norm.

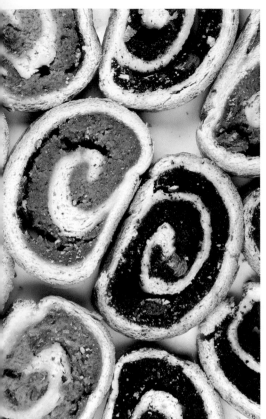

Hungarian beigli, with poppy seed or walnut fillings, are special treats.

Most Hungarians rarely go to restaurants, except on very special occasions, such as weddings or the annual office celebration. They prefer to eat at home and go out only for pastry and coffee, or for a drink.

The midday meal is traditionally the main meal and is generally eaten at work or school, in a cafeteria. Supper may be a soup, leftovers, or cold meats, served with cheese, bread, tomatoes, and peppers. Weekend midday meals and evening suppers with guests usually involve the preparation of several courses. The table setting is informal, and the company may eat in more than one sitting if there are too many guests for the small table. Good manners are still expected when eating, and small children (or sloppy adults) are quickly reprimanded if they eat loudly or carelessly.

CAKES, PASTRIES, AND SWEETS

The Hungarian *cukrászda* (TSOO-krahs-dah), or pastry shop, is a palace of wonders. It's filled with creamy delicacies like *Rigó Jancsi* (REE-goh-yahn-chee), a chocolate-flavored jelly roll sandwiched with chocolate custard and cream, or *gesztenye püré* (GEH-stehn-yeh PYU-rai), a chestnut puree with whipped cream. Poppy seeds are in many different Hungarian confections—from pastries and bread pudding to noodles eaten with poppy seeds and sugar. Coffee (*kávé*) was first brought to Hungary by the Turks. It is generally prepared espresso-style and served with milk, cream, whipped cream, or sugar.

Another characteristic Hungarian delight, and a favorite of children, is *palacsinta* (PAH-lah-chin-tah), a rolled crepe filled with jam, chocolate powder, syrup, cottage cheese, sweetened nuts, or an elaborate mixture of several of these. (There is also a savory variety, filled with *pörkölt* or cabbage.) Palacsinta is not available in bakeries, but at special stands in resorts, parks, and other places where Hungarians go to relax.

FAST FOOD

Political changes and the influx of Western businesses, habits, and tastes have begun to affect the Hungarian diet. Traditional kinds of fast food, including *lángos* (LAHNG-gohsh), a plate-size piece of deep-fried dough made from potatoes and topped with salt, garlic, sour cream, and grated cheese; sausage; corn-on-the-cob; and fried fish have been around for years, later augmented by *hamburgerek* and *hotdogok* ("hamburgers" and "hot dogs").

But the arrival of McDonald's in 1988, followed by a host of other American chains with their flashy advertisements, English-language signs, and shiny outlets, has introduced a new generation of Hungarians to the international fast food culture. These are not the cheapest places to eat; one meal in a fast food restaurant costs more than a meal in most traditional restaurants. Those who eat there regularly tend to be young and affluent urban Hungarians, many of whom use these places to meet their friends.

When McDonald's first opened in Budapest, customers lined up outside to sample this exotic Western cuisine.

INTERNET LINKS

easteuropeanfood.about.com/od/flavorsofeasterneurope/tp/10-Hungarian-Recipes.htm
"Ten Reasons to Try Hungarian Food" has ten favorite recipes with links.

allrecipes.com/recipes/world-cuisine/european/eastern-european/hungarian
Hungarian recipes in American measures are available on this site.

HIDEG MEGGYLEVES
(HUNGARIAN COLD SOUR CHERRY SOUP)

This soup is refreshing on a hot summer day.

2 lbs. fresh sour cherries, pitted (Morello cherries are best, but any red sour cherry is fine. Only use bing, or sweet cherries as a last resort; the flavor won't be the same.)
1 cup water or cherry juice
2 Tbsp sugar (or more to taste)
½ tsp salt
1 cinnamon stick
1 thick slice lemon, seeded
½—1 cup sour cream, to taste
1 Tbsp flour

Place cherries, juice (or water) sugar, salt, cinnamon stick, and lemon slice in a saucepan. Bring to a boil, reduce heat to low, and simmer until the cherries are tender, about 10 minutes.

Let cool, then discard the lemon and cinnamon.

Remove ½ cup of the cherries with a slotted spoon and puree the remaining mixture with an immersion blender or regular blender until smooth.

Whisk flour into sour cream. If the soup is still hot, add a few spoonfuls to the sour cream mixture to temper it. Then whisk the sour cream into the soup until smooth. Simmer lightly for 5 minutes, but do not boil.

Add the reserved cherries back to the mixture, cover the bowl with plastic wrap, and refrigerate several hours or overnight until thoroughly chilled. Serve cold. Serves 4—6.

PAPRIKAS CSIRKE (CHICKEN PAPRIKASH)

This dish is great on a cold winter's night.

8 chicken pieces (thighs are good), or one whole chicken, cut up
salt, black pepper
3 Tbsp butter
2 yellow onions, sliced
2—3 Tbsp Hungarian sweet paprika
½ tsp —1 tsp cayenne pepper
1 cup chicken broth
2 bay leaves
1 tomato, cubed
1 cup chopped green pepper
2 Tbsp flour
½—1 cup sour cream

Pat chicken dry with paper towels and season with salt and black pepper.

In a large, wide pot, melt the butter over medium heat. Add chicken pieces skin-side down in the pan. Brown for about 10 minutes, turning, until it is well browned on both sides. Remove chicken to a plate. Lower the heat and add the onions. Cook until translucent but not brown.

To the pan, add the paprika, cayenne pepper, broth, tomato, green pepper, and bay leaves, stirring to mix. Nestle the chicken pieces into the pan on top of the mixture. Cover and cook on a low simmer for 20—25 minutes. Once the chicken pieces are cooked through, remove the pan from heat.

Remove the chicken from the pan. Mix flour into the sour cream, and then whisk sour cream mixture into the sauce in the pan. Simmer lightly just until thickened. Do not boil.

Add the chicken back to the pan and coat with the sauce. Serve the chicken with dumplings, egg noodles, or rice. Serves 4—6.

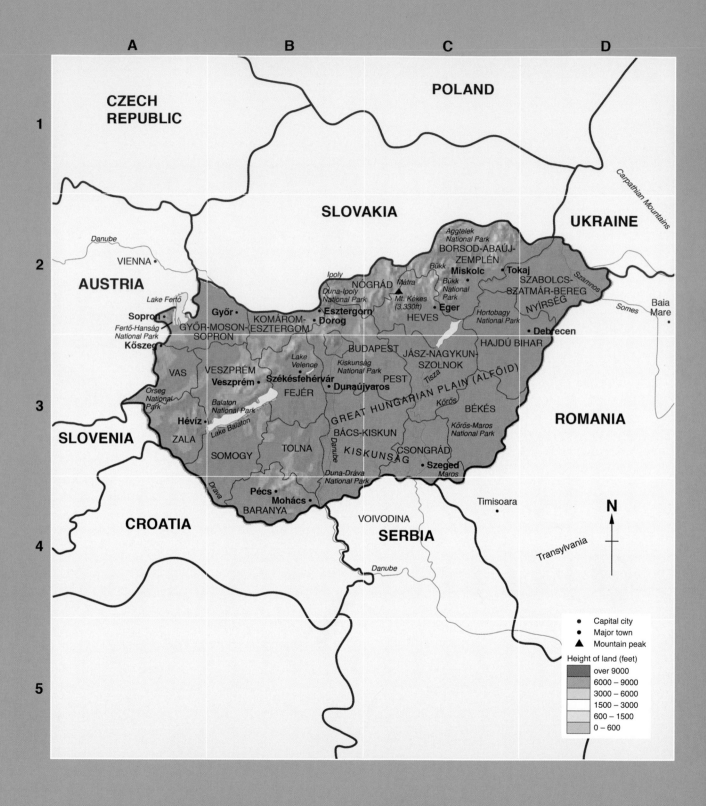

A · B · C · D

CZECH
REPUBLIC

POLAND

1

SLOVAKIA

UKRAINE

Danube

VIENNA ·

2

AUSTRIA

Lake Fertő

Aggtelek
National Park

BORSOD-ABAÚJ-
ZEMPLÉN

Bükk

Miskolc   · Tokaj

Ipoly

NÓGRÁD   *Mátra*

SZABOLCS-
SZATMÁR-BEREG

Szamos

Sopron ·

Duna-Ipoly
National Park

Bükk
Bükk
National
Park

NYÍRSÉG

Somes

Baia
Mare

Fertő-Hanság
National Park

Győr ·

KOMÁROM-
ESZTERGOM

· Esztergom
· Dorog

Mt. Kékes
(3,330ft)

· Eger

HEVES

Hortobagy
National Park

· Debrecen

Kőszeg ·

GYŐR-MOSON-
SOPRON

HAJDÚ BIHAR

VAS

VESZPRÉM

*Lake
Velence*

BUDAPEST

JÁSZ-NAGYKUN-
SZOLNOK

GREAT HUNGARIAN PLAIN (ALFÖLD)

Tisza

Orseg
National
Park

Veszprém ·

· Székésfehérvár

Kiskunság
National Park

· Dunaújvaros

PEST

3

FEJÉR

*Balaton
National
Park*

BÉKÉS

Hévíz ·

Lake Balaton

Körös

SLOVENIA

ZALA

SOMOGY

TOLNA

Duna

KISKUNSÁG

Körös-Maros
National Park

ROMANIA

BÁCS-KISKUN

CSONGRÁD

Drava

Duna-Dráva
National Park

· Szeged

Maros

Pécs ·

· Mohács

BARANYA

Timisoara
·

CROATIA

VOIVODINA

SERBIA

N

4

Transylvania

Danube

5

Capital city
Major town
▲ Mountain peak

Height of land (feet)
over 9000
6000 – 9000
3000 – 6000
1500 – 3000
600 – 1500
0 – 600

Carpathian Mountains

MAP OF HUNGARY

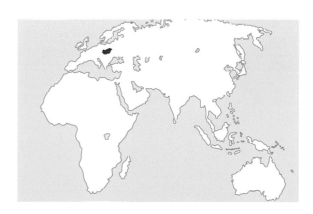

ECONOMIC HUNGARY

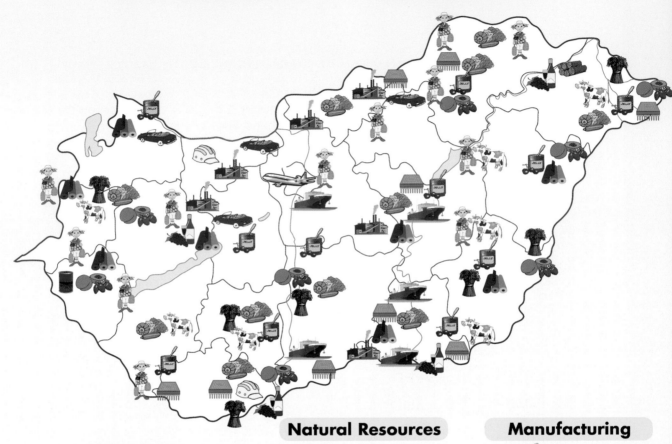

Agriculture

 Crops

Fishery

Fruits

Livestock

Vegetables

Vineyards

Natural Resources

Mining

Oil Refinery

Timber

Services

Airport

Port

Tourism

Manufacturing

Heavy Industry

Light Industry

Processed Foods

Textiles

Vehicles

ABOUT THE ECONOMY

OVERVIEW

Hungary has made the transition from a centrally planned economy to a market economy, with a per capita income of only two-thirds the EU average. In late 2008, the global financial crisis led Budapest to obtain an IMF/EU/World Bank-arranged financial assistance package worth over $25 billion. In 2013, Hungary's improved economic performance, and progress reducing its deficit led the European Commission to permit Hungary to exit the Excessive Deficit Procedure for the first time since joining the EU in 2004, but Hungary still faces many challenges. Low-skilled labor supply greatly exceeds demand, especially in disadvantaged regions. Education outcomes are relatively good on average, but the poor performance of disadvantaged students, notably Roma, limits their employment prospects and social mobility.

GROSS DOMESTIC PRODUCT (GDP)

US$130.6 billion (2013)

GDP SECTORS

Services 68.7 percent, industry 28 percent, agriculture 3.4 percent (2013)

INFLATION RATE

1.9 percent (2013)

LABOR FORCE

4.3 million (2013)

CURRENCY

Hungarian forint (HUF)
Notes: 200; 500; 1,000; 2,000; 5,000; 10,000 forint. Coins: 1, 2, 5, 10, 20, 50, 100, and 200 forint
1 Hungarian forint = .0037 US dollar
1 US dollar = 273.94 Hungarian forint (January 2015)

LABOR FORCE BY OCCUPATION

Services 63.2 percent, industry 29.7 percent, agriculture 7.1 percent (2013)

UNEMPLOYMENT RATE

10.5 percent (2013)

AGRICULTURAL PRODUCTS

Wheat, corn, sunflower seed, potatoes, sugar beets, poppy, pigs, cattle, poultry, dairy products

INDUSTRIES

Mining, metallurgy, construction materials, processed foods, textiles, chemicals (especially pharmaceuticals), motor vehicles

MAJOR TRADE PARTNERS

Germany, Russia, China, Austria, Slovakia, France, Italy, Poland, Romania, the Netherlands, UK

PORTS AND HARBORS

Budapest, Dunaujvaros

CULTURAL HUNGARY

Benedictine Church
Built in the 1300s, the Benedictine Church in Sopron, is commonly called the "Goat Church." According to legend, a goatherd financed the church's construction with loot unearthed by his animals. Three kings were crowned in the church and Parliament convened here on seven occasions.

Bust of St. László
Within Gyor is the gilded silver bust of St. László, housed in the Gothic Hederváry Chapel (of St. Ladislaus). It is considered the finest example of the craft of medieval Hungarian goldsmiths. Other masterpieces of a thousand years of ecclesiastic art can also be viewed in the city.

Aquincum
Aquincum was originally a Celtic settlement in the Óbuda sector of Budapest. The Romans made it the provincial capital of Pannonia Inferior. The remains of the foundation walls and the underground piping provide visitors with an idea of Aquincum's layout.

The Minorite Church
Built in 1771, the Minorite Church in the old Magyar settlement of Eger is one of the most stunning examples of baroque architecture in Hungary and in Central Europe. Statues of city's heroic defenders, who fought off the Turks in 1552, fill the square in front of the church.

The Great Calvinist Church
The neoclassical Great Calvinist Church in Debrecen housed the Diet of 1849 that proclaimed Hungary's independence-the church's prized possession is the armchair of Lajos Kossuth, who made the declaration. Debrecen is where Calvinism took root and the Great Calvinist Church is the largest Calvinist church in Hungary.

Lake Balaton
Also called "The Hungarian Sea," there are endless things to do at and around the lake with its 25 lakeside resorts; medicinal baths and lakes; vineyards; extinct volcanoes; Roman, medieval, and Hungarian monuments; museums; parks; country walks; fishing spots; galleries; ferries; bird sanctuaries; churches and monastries; and caves.

Mosque of Pasha Ghazi Qassim
With its green domes, ornate window grilles, and scalloped niches, the Mosque of Pasha Ghazi Oassim in Pees is one ol the finest examples of Islamic architecture in Hungary. The vaulted interior and Islamic prayer niche are decorated in Arabic calligraphy. Built from the stones of a Gothic church, it functions today as a Catholic church.

St. Stephen's Basilica
St. Stephen's Basilica in Szekesfehervár was the most important building in Hungary between the 11th and 16th centuries. Here, 37 kings and 39 queens were crowned, and 15 monarchs buried. The Holy Crown and State Archi ves were once kept here, and national assemblies gathered here. Blown up by the Turks in 1602, the Hungarians rebuilt the church in the 18th century. The original foundations can be seen in the "Garden of Ruins," which also houses King Stephen's sarcophagus.

ABOUT THE CULTURE

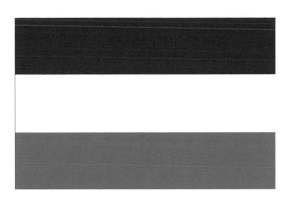

OFFICIAL NAME
The Republic of Hungary

CAPITAL
Budapest

OTHER MAJOR CITIES
Debrecen, Miskolc, Szeged, Pécs, and Györ

POPULATION
9,919,128 (2014)

GOVERNMENT
Parliamentary democracy

NATIONAL FLAG
Three equal bands in red (strength), white (fidelity), and green (hope). The national colors first appeared in 1618 on a seal ribbon during the reign of King Matthias II.

NATIONAL ANTHEM
The Anthem (*Himnusz*). Written by Ferenc Kölcsey in 1823; set to music by Ferenc Erkel in 1844.

LITERACY RATE
99 percent

ETHNIC GROUPS
Hungarian 92.3 percent, Roma 1.9 percent, others or unknown, 5.8 percent. (2001)

RELIGIOUS GROUPS
Roman Catholic 37.2 percent, Calvinist 11.6 percent, Lutheran 2.2 percent, Greek Catholic 1.8 percent, other 1.9 percent, none 18.2 percent, unspecified 27.2 percent (2011)

LIFE EXPECTANCY AT BIRTH
male: 71.7 years
female: 79.4 years (2014)

IMPORTANT ANNIVERSARIES
Start of the 1848–49 War of Independence (March 15), Saint Stephen's Day (August 20), Anniversary of the 1956 Revolution & Day of the Proclamation of the Republic of Hungary (October 23)

LEADERS IN POLITICS
Janos Ader, president (2012—)
Viktor Orban, prime minister, (2014—)

TIMELINE

IN HUNGARY	IN THE WORLD
1000–500 BCE • Hungarians become a distinct ethnic group; the ethnic name "magyar" first appears.	
	• **753 BCE** Rome is founded.
	• **116–17 BCE** The Roman Empire reaches its greatest extent, under Emperor Trajan (98–17).
895–96 CE • Magyars arrive in the Carpathian Basin.	
	• **600 CE** Height of Mayan civilization.
1000 • Coronation of King Stephen I.	• **1000** The Chinese perfect gunpowder and begin to use it in warfare.
1456 • Janos Hunyadi defeats the Turkish army at Nandorfehervar.	
1526 • The Turkish army conquers Hungary. Hungary is partitioned into three.	
	• **1530** Beginning of trans-Atlantic slave trade organized by the Portuguese in Africa.
	• **1558–1603** Reign of Elizabeth I of England
	• **1620** Pilgrims sail the *Mayflower* to America.
1686 • Holy League armies recapture Buda from the Turks.	
1703–11 • The war of liberation from Habsburg rule.	
1781 • Joseph II decrees the free exercise of religion in the Edict of Toleration.	• **1776** US Declaration of Independence.
	• **1789–99** The French Revolution.
1848–49 • The Hungarian War of Independence.	
1867 • The Compromise of 1867 leads to the creation of the Austro-Hungarian monarchy.	• **1861** The US Civil War begins.
	• **1869** The Suez Canal is opened.
	• **1914** World War I begins.
1920 • The Trianon Peace Treaty is signed.	

IN HUNGARY	IN THE WORLD
	• 1939 World War II begins.
1941 • Hungary enters World War II against the Soviet Union.	
1944 • Hungary is occupied by the Germans.	
1945 • The Soviets occupy Hungary. The first free elections are won by the Smallholders' Party.	**• 1945** The United States drops atomic bombs on Hiroshima and Nagasaki.
1947 • The Paris Peace Treaty is signed. The Communist Party secures the majority vote.	**• 1949** The North Atlantic Treaty Organization (NATO) is formed.
1956 • The October 23 Revolution takes place.	**• 1957** The Russians launch *Sputnik*.
	• 1969 The Chinese Cultural Revolution.
	• 1986 Nuclear power disaster at Chernobyl in Ukraine.
1989 • Imre Nagy and his fellow martyrs of 1956 are reburied. Hungary opens its border to East German refugees	
1990 • The first free multiparty elections held.	**• 1991** Break-up of the Soviet Union.
1999 • Hungary is admitted to NATO.	
	• 2001 Terrorists crash planes in New York; Washington, DC; and Pennsylvania.
2004 • Hungary joins the European Union.	**• 2003** War in Iraq.
2011 • Parliament approves new constitution.	
2014 • Conservative ruling party Fidesz wins second victory. Thousands rally in Budapest protesting official corruption.	**• 2014** Russia invades Ukraine.

GLOSSARY

beigli (BAY-glee)
A rolled Christmas pastry filled with poppy seeds or walnuts.

busójarás (BOO-shoh-yah-rahsh)
The Busójárás Festival celebrates the last day before the start of Lent and the end of winter.

címer (TSEE-mehr)
Hungary's coat-of-arms.

csikós (CHEE-kohsh)
Hungarian cowboy.

collectivization
The process by which the Communist government forced private farmers off their land and into large communal farms.

communism
A political, economic, and social system in which all property and resources are collectively owned by the state, and wealth is distributed—theoretically—equally or according to need.

cukrászda
A pastry shop

feudal landholding
A system in which the land the peasant works does not belong to him completely.

gimnázium (GIM-nah-zee-uhm)
academic high school

lakótelep (LAH-koh-teh-lep)
a high-rise apartment complex

Magyars
ethnic Hungarians

nationalism
an emotional form of patriotism that asserts the superiority of one's own country and countrymen

pálinka (PAH-lin-kah)
brandy made from pear, apricot, or cherry

piac (PEE-ahts)
a fruit and vegetable market, or flea market

populism
a 1930s political movement to improve conditions of the peasantry

proletariat
industrial working class

puszta (POO-stah)
Hungarian plain

virsli (VEER-shlee)
pork sausages

FOR FURTHER INFORMATION

BOOKS

Bori, Istvan. *The Essential Guide to Being Hungarian*. North Adams, MA: New Europe Books, 2012

Turp, Craig. *Eyewitness Travel Guide: Hungary*. New York: Dorling Kindersley Publishing, 2013

Gergely, Aniko. *Culinaria*. Potsdam, Germany: H.F. Ullman Publishing, 2013

Kor, Eva Mozes and Lisa Rojany Buccieri, *Surviving the Angel of Death: The True Story of a Mengele Twin in Auschwitz*. Terre Haute, IN: Tanglewood, 2011 (Young adult)

Lendvai, Paul. *The Hungarians: A Thousand Years of Victory in Defeat*. Princeton, NJ: Princeton University Press, 2003.

McLean, Brian. *Hungary: Culture Smart! a quick guide to customs & etiquette*. London: Kuperard, 2006.

Mitchener, James A. *The Bridge at Andau: The Compelling True Story of a Brave, Embattled People*. New York: Random House, 1957; Dial Press 2014. (classic historical fiction about the Hungarian Revolution)

Siegal, Aranka. *Upon the Head of the Goat: A Childhood in Hungary 1939—1944*. New York: Puffin Books, 2003. (Young adult, Newberry Honor Book)

WEBSITES

Allrecipes.com. Hungarian Recipes. allrecipes.com/recipes/world cuisine/european/eastern -european/hungarian

CIA. "The World Factbook: Hungary." www.cia.gov/library/publications/the-world-factbook /geos/hu.html

Hungarian Tourism: Go to Hungary. gotohungary.com/about-hungary

Hungarian government. www.kormany.hu/en

International Commission for the Protection of the Danube River. "Hungary." www.icpdr.org /main/danube-basin/hungary

Jewish Virtual Library, "The Jewish Virtual World: Hungary." www.jewishvirtuallibrary.org /jsource/vjw/Hungary.html

Lonely Planet: Hungary. www.lonelyplanet.com/hungary

National Geographic: Budapest, Hungary. travel.nationalgeographic.com/travel/city-guides /budapest-hungary

FILM

In the Footsteps of Liszt. Kultur Video, 2012 (DVD)

Szabó, István. *Mephisto*. Anchor Bay Entertainment, 2001 (DVD)

BIBLIOGRAPHY

BIBLIOGRAPHY

A.L.B., "Roma in Hungary: A terrible waste of human potential." *The Economist*, Aug. 7, 2013.
www.economist.com/blogs/easternapproaches/2013/08/roma-hungary

BBC News Hungary Profile, Timeline. www.bbc.com/news/world-europe-17383522

Blumgart, Jake. "Hungary After Communism." *Jacobin*, Jan. 7, 2014.
www.jacobinmag.com/2014/01/hungary-after-communism

CIA. "The World Factbook: Hungary."
www.cia.gov/library/publications/the-world-factbook/geos/hu.html

Faris, Stephen. "Power Hungary: How Viktor Orban Became Europe's New Strongman."
Businessweek, Jan. 22, 2015. www.businessweek.com/articles/2015-01-22/power-hungary-
viktor-orban-europe-s-new-strongman

Hess, Alexander E.M., Thomas C. Frolich and Vince Calio. "The Heaviest-Drinking Countries
in the World," 24/7 Wall St, May 15, 2014. 247wallst.com/special-report/2014/05/15/the-
heaviest-drinking-countries-in-the-world

Hungarian government. www.kormany.hu/en

International Commission for the Protection of the Danube River. "Hungary." www.icpdr.org

Jewish Virtual Library, "The Jewish Virtual World: Hungary."
www.jewishvirtuallibrary.org/jsource/vjw/Hungary.html

Lyman, Rick and Alison Smale. "Viktor Orban Steers Hungary Toward Russia 25 Years After Fall
of the Berlin Wall." *The New York Times*, Nov. 7, 2014. www.nytimes.com/2014/11/08/world/
europe/viktor-orban-steers-hungary-toward-russia-25-years-after-fall-of-the-berlin-wall.html

Meyerson, Harold. "Hungary's prime minister a champion for illiberalism." *The Washington
Post*, Aug. 6, 2014. www.washingtonpost.com/opinions/harold-meyerson-hungarys-
prime-minister-is-a-champion-of-illiberalism/2014/08/06/143a53ae-1d9d-11e4-82f9-
2cd6fa8da5c4_story.html

Nadler, John. "Why Hungary's New Constitution Could Be Bad for Europe." Time, Jan.5, 2012
content.time.com/time/world/article/0,8599,2103775,00.html

_____"Why Hungary's Youth Are Angry—and Drifting to the Far Right." *Time*, March 7,
2012 content.time.com/time/world/article/0,8599,2108389,00.html

NPR staff. "How Franz Liszt Became the World's First Rock Star." NPR, Oct. 22, 2011. www.npr.
org/2011/10/22/141617637/how-franz-liszt-became-the-worlds-first-rock-star

Webster, George. "The little cube that changed the world." CNN, Oct. 11, 2012.
www.cnn.com/2012/10/10/tech/rubiks-cube-inventor

Woodruff, Sasa. "Increased Hostility Against Jews And Roma In Hungary." NPR, March 9, 2014
www.npr.org/blogs/codeswitch/2014/03/09/287342069/increased-hostility-against-jews-
and-roma-in-hungary

INDEX

INDEX